sophia

52 Week Devotional
for Girls Ages 6-9

An imprint of Rose Publishing, Inc.
Carson, CA
www.Rose-Publishing.com

52 Week Devotional
for Girls Ages 6-9

Diane Cory
Kathy Widenhouse

Compiled from GOD and ME!® Devotional for Girls 6-9 series, vols. 1-3
(Carson, CA: Rose Publishing, ©2012-2015)

GOD and ME!® 52 WEEK DEVOTIONAL FOR GIRLS AGES 6-9
Compilation copyright ©2016 by Rose Publishing, Inc.
ISBN 10: 1-58411-177-1
ISBN 13: 978-1-58411-177-1
RoseKidz® reorder# L46838
JUVENILE NONFICTION/Religion/Devotion & Prayer

RoseKidz®
An imprint of Rose Publishing, Inc.
17909 Adria Maru Lane
Carson, CA 90746
www.Rose-Publishing.com

Unless otherwise indicated, Scripture quotations are from THE HOLY BIBLE, NEW INTERNATIONAL VERSION®, NIV® Copyright © 1973, 1978, 1984, 2011 by Biblica, Inc.® Used by permission. All rights reserved worldwide.

Verses marked NLT are from the Holy Bible. New Living Translation copyright© 1996, 2004, 2007, 2013 by Tyndale House Foundation. Used by permission of Tyndale House Publishers Inc., Carol Stream, Illinois 60188. All rights reserved.

Cover and interior design by Nancy L. Haskins
Illustrations by Aline L. Heiser and Dave Carleson

All rights reserved. No part of this publication may be reproduced in any form, stored in a retrieval system, or transmitted in any form or by any means without the written permission of Rose Publishing.

Printed in South Korea   02   08.2016.APC

Table of Contents

Table of Contents

Best Friends!

Hey, girls! Do you know God wants to be *your* very special friend? He knows everything about you, and He wants you to know Him. This hands-on devotional book will help you discover God and His ways. You'll also find out that as you learn to live God's way, He will point you toward making the best choices in your daily life.

Living God's way is different than living your own way. That's why it's so important to learn to live His way. When we love God, He helps us learn to obey Him even when we don't want to at first. Living His way is the perfect way to be happy!

If there are words or ideas you find hard to understand, ask your parents or another adult to help you. If you're just learning to read, ask your parents, another family member, or an adult you trust to read this book with you. Puzzle answers are at the back of the book.

You can read the devotionals in this book whenever you want and in whatever order you like. Memorize each week's Bible verse and don't forget to pray! Ask God to help you use what you learn. Remember to listen for God's voice in your heart and mind.

Being friends with God is awesome, SO LET'S GET STARTED!

God Wants You to Know Him

I am the LORD; that is my name!
I will not yield my glory to another or my praise to idols.

– Isaiah 42:8

God Shows Himself in the Bible

"What's your name?"

"My name is Sally. I live in the yellow house on the corner."

"It's nice to meet you, Sally. My name is Tracy. I live in the blue house by the park."

When you first meet people, it is good to find out their names and tell them yours. How do you explain to others who you are? If you tell them your name, you share one of the most important things about you. By trading names, you are sharing about yourself.

God tells about Himself in the Bible. In today's verse, God is introducing Himself. He wants you to know Him as well as you know your own family.

God already knows everything about you. He knows you so well that "even the very hairs of your head are all numbered" (Matthew 10:30). However, God loves to listen to *you* talk to Him. He likes it when *you* share about yourself.

Your Turn

1. How do you tell people who you are?
2. How does God tell you who He is?
3. How can you tell your friends about God?

1 Say your name. 2 Through the bible. 3 Invite them to church.

Prayer

Thank You, God, for helping me to know who You are. I'm glad to know you! Amen.

9

God Wants You to Know Him

I am the LORD; that is my name!
I will not yield my glory to another or my praise to idols.

– Isaiah 42:8

The Contact List

Fill out these contact pages with the names of your friends and family. Pray for each person every day.

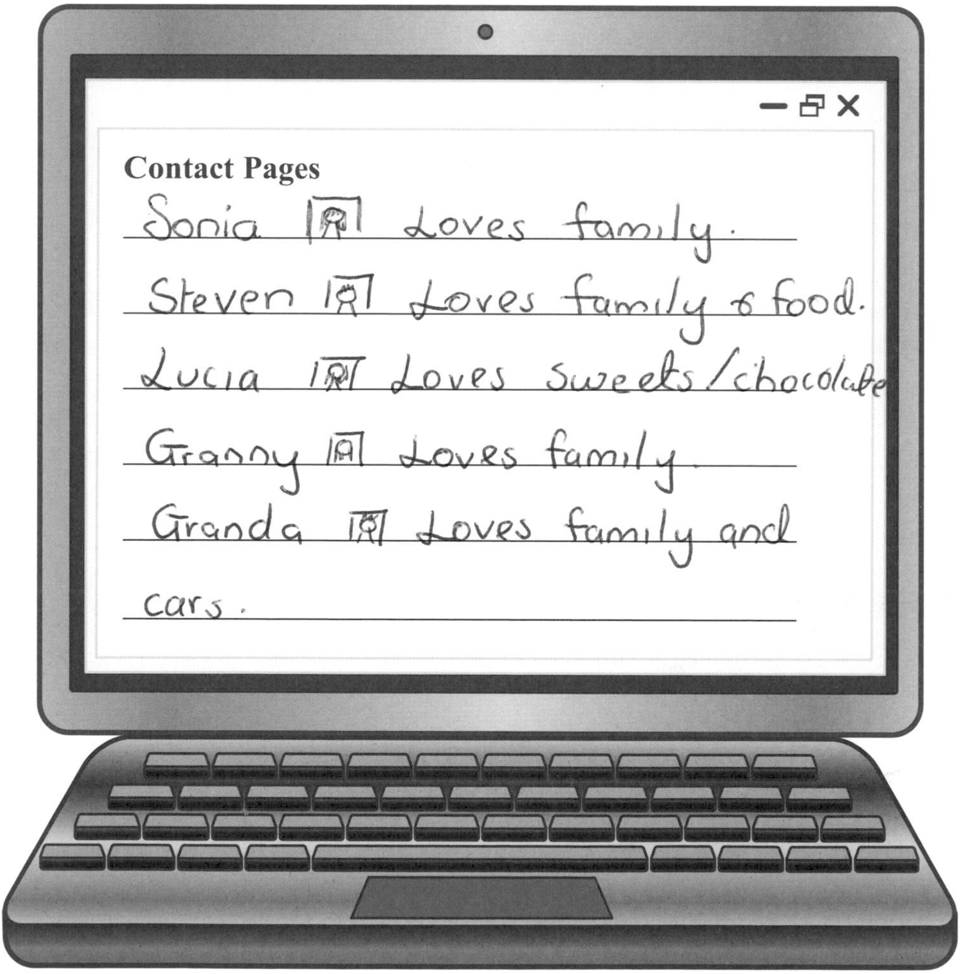

Contact Pages

Sonia ⬚ Loves family.

Steven ⬚ Loves family & food.

Lucia ⬚ Loves sweets/chocolate

Granny ⬚ Loves family.

Granda ⬚ Loves family and

cars.

Prayer

Dear God, help me remember to pray for my family and friends every day. Amen.

God Wants You to Know Him

I am the LORD; that is my name!
I will not yield my glory to another or my praise to idols.

– Isaiah 42:8

Name Squares Puzzle

Write your name going down the squares, each letter going in a square. Make new boxes if you need to. Use each letter as the start of a different word that tells about you.

S   mart ?

o   bidient . ?

p   retty ?

h   ealthy

i   nocent .

a   ~~mas~~ mazing

Prayer

Thank You, God, for my name. Teach me more about Your name. I want to know You better, and I want to tell people about You. Amen.

God Wants You to Know Him

I am the LORD; that is my name!
I will not yield my glory to another or my praise to idols.

– Isaiah 42:8

The Bible Tells What God Is Like

The day you were born was a happy day for your parents. Before you came home from the hospital, they signed a birth certificate. A birth certificate tells about you. It has your name and your parents' names. It also tells the time and place you were born.

Do you think God has a birth certificate? No! Why? Because God was not born. He does not have an age. He has always been! Your birth certificate tells who you are and some other things about you. But God tells us His names and other things about Him in His Word, the Bible.

The Bible tells us who God is—God has many names that help us to know Him. He is called Immanuel ("God with us"). He is also called the Good Shepherd. The Bible also tells what God does. It tells us that He is the Creator of everything. He sees and hears us. And the Bible says He always loves us. He never changes His mind about that!

Your Turn

1. What are some things the Bible tells us about God?
2. What is something you would like to know about God?

He sent his son Jesus to die on the cross
for us to take away ow our sins.
Why that even though we sin he still
loves us and sent his son!

Prayer

I thank You, God, for the Bible. Your Word tells me who *You* are and what *You* are like. Help me remember to read Your Word each day. Amen.

God Wants You to Know Him

I am the LORD; that is my name!
I will not yield my glory to another or my praise to idols.

– Isaiah 42:8

Family Art

Draw a picture of a family member's nose, ears, mouth, and eyes. Ask your mother, father, or grandparents to share some family pictures with you.

Prayer

Thank You, God, for creating me just the way I am! Amen.

God Wants You to Know Him

I am the LORD; that is my name!
I will not yield my glory to another or my praise to idols.

– Isaiah 42:8

Naming the Stars

Did you know that God has a name for every star? It's true! Psalm 147:4 tells that He chose how many stars to make and calls each one by name.

Draw stars in the frame. Give each one a name. Then look for stars tonight!

Prayer

God, I see Your work in the night sky. Thank You for being my God. Amen.

God Wants You to Know Him

*I am the L*ORD*; that is my name!*
I will not yield my glory to another or my praise to idols.

– Isaiah 42:8

Family Apple Tree

Write the names of family members on the apples. Put your mother's family on one side of the tree. Put your father's family on the other side of the tree. Let this family apple tree remind you that the same God who created apple trees also created you and your family.

Prayer

God, thank You for making all Your creations, and my family, too.
Amen.

God Sees Things You Can't

You are the God who sees me.
– Genesis 16:13

God Sees Everything

Do you know people who wear glasses to see better? Without glasses they have a hard time reading texts and even road signs. But God never needs glasses. He is the God who sees everything.

Can you see a movie and your grandmother at the same time? God can!

When you stand on the shore of a lake or ocean, look down into the water. Can you see fish swimming at the bottom? God can!

Your Turn

1. What are some good things God sees when He looks at you?
2. What are some not-so-good things you think God sees?
3. What could you ask God to help you change?

1. Nice smile, Good and kind heart, Good family, play sports and love him. 2. I sin, I annoy my sister and I sometimes don't take time to pray. 3. Ask him to help me pray more.

Prayer

LORD, I love You. I am glad You see me and want me to know You. Stop me when You see I am headed for trouble. Amen.

God Sees Things You Can't

You are the God who sees me.

– Genesis 16:13

The Giant Eyeglasses

Draw a picture of yourself in one lens. Draw a picture of your family in the other lens. Remember, God lovingly sees you and your family.

Here's another idea. Point to what you see and say, "God sees the trees," and "God sees the birds," and "God sees the cars."

Prayer

LORD, thank You that You see me and that You love me. Amen.

God Sees Things You Can't

You are the God who sees me.

– Genesis 16:13

My Psalm to God Who Sees Me

Read Psalm 139:2. A psalm is like a song for God. Write your own psalm by adding your own words.

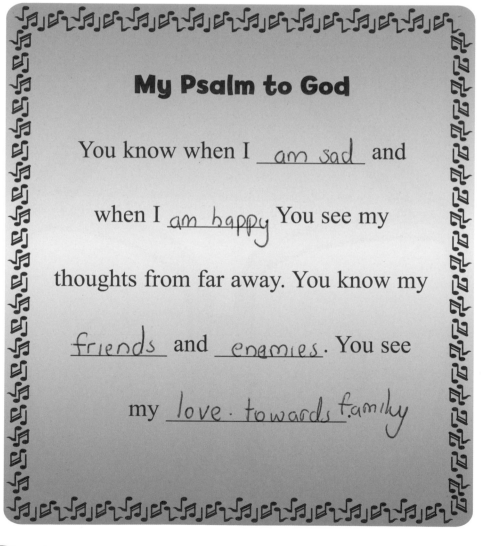

My Psalm to God

You know when I _am sad_ and

when I _am happy_ You see my

thoughts from far away. You know my

friends and _enemies_. You see

my _love towards family_

Prayer

Thank You, God, for watching me and loving me. Amen.

God Sees Things You Can't

You are the God who sees me.
– Genesis 16:13

God Cares About Your Feelings

Do you live in an apartment or a house? The place you live is your *home.* Your home is where you stay.

Your heart is like your home for your feelings. Your heart is where your feelings live. Love or hate can live in your heart-home. A hug can make your heart feel happy. A clap of thunder can make your heart feel afraid. Your sister playing in your room without asking might make your heart mad.

God sees everything in your heart. He looks in your heart because He loves you. God wants to cheer you when you are sad. He wants to rejoice with you when you are happy. God will comfort you when you are afraid. He cares about *all* of your feelings.

Your Turn

1. What makes you feel afraid?
2. When God sees your afraid feelings, how does He help you?

1. Darkness and hights. & and corona
2. I pray and he takes my fears and bad thoughts away.

Prayer

God, You look inside my heart. I know I can ask You for help, joy, and comfort. Thank You. Amen.

God Sees Things You Can't

You are the God who sees me.

– Genesis 16:13

A Heart List

Make a list of your feelings inside the heart house. Talk to God about each one of them.

My Feelings List

1.

2.

3.

WELCOME!

Prayer

Thank You, God, that You are always with me to help me when I am afraid or sad. Amen.

God Sees Things You Can't

You are the God who sees me.

– Genesis 16:13

My Flag for God

If you were going to fly a flag to let people know you love God, what would it look like? Make a heart flag of love for God on the flag pole. Decorate it so people know you love God.

Prayer

God, I want to love You more. I want You to see my love for You in my heart and in my actions. Amen.

God Sees Things You Can't

You are the God who sees me.

– Genesis 16:13

My Daily Diary

At the end of each day this week, write down the things God saw you do that day. Then talk to Him about it.

Monday:
_____

Tuesday:
_____

Wednesday:
_____

Thursday:
_____

Friday:
_____

Saturday:
_____

Sunday:
_____

Prayer

Dear God, help me obey You in everything I do and say. Let me know when I am doing something wrong and help me change. Amen.

God Never Changes

Jesus Christ is the same yesterday and today and forever.
– Hebrews 13:8

The Four Seasons

Spring, summer, fall, and winter. There are four seasons in a year. Each season brings changes. For instance in the fall, school usually starts. The leaves on many trees change color and fall to the ground.

Winter brings cold, rain, and snow. There is a chill in the air. Ice skating and sledding are great activities.

Spring brings buds to the tips of plants and baby animals are born.

Summer is hot and perfect for swimming and in-line skating. Butterflies show up, and many families go on vacation because school is out.

The seasons change, but God never changes.

Your Turn

1. Look outside. Name the changes you see right now.
2. How do you know that God never changes?

_____

_____

_____

_____

_____

_____

Prayer

God, thank You that Your love for me never changes. Amen.

God Never Changes

Jesus Christ is the same yesterday and today and forever.

– Hebrews 13:8

Skating Through the Seasons

Draw a line along the path as the girls are in-line skating through the seasons. Along the path, write a way you change in each season. For example, maybe you keep your hair longer in the winter.

Prayer

Thank You, God, that even though things change in my life, I can always count on You to always love me. Amen.

God Never Changes

Jesus Christ is the same yesterday and today and forever.
– Hebrews 13:8

The Time Machine

Use the keyboard code to decipher the secret message in the time machine.
You will discover a truth about God.

| 25 | 15 | 21 |

| 18 | 5 | 13 | 1 | 9 | 14 |

| 20 | 8 | 5 | | 19 | 1 | 13 | 5 | , |

| 7 | 15 | 4 |

A	B	C	D	E	F	G	H	I
1	2	3	4	5	6	7	8	9

J	K	L	M	N	O	P	Q	R
10	11	12	13	14	15	16	17	18

S	T	U	V	W	X	Y	Z
19	20	21	22	23	24	25	26

Prayer

Dear LORD, thank You that You are always the same. I can trust You always. Amen.

25

God Never Changes

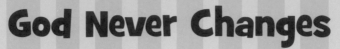

Jesus Christ is the same yesterday and today and forever.
– Hebrews 13:8

You Change but God Doesn't

Imagine it is five years from now. What do you think you will look like? What might be different about your room? Your school? Do you think you will like the same food and books and movies?

God can see what you will be like in five years. He knows how you will change. But He never changes, no matter how much time goes by.

Your Turn

1. What are things you hope will be better about you five years from now?
2. How does it make you feel to know that God does not change?

_____

_____

_____

_____

_____

_____

Prayer

I'm so glad You never change, God. Help me change the things I do that make You sad. Amen.

God Never Changes

Jesus Christ is the same yesterday and today and forever.
– Hebrews 13:8

The Gift Box

Inside this gift box, write or draw things you can give to God, like praise and love. Decorate the outside of the box. Look at the box tomorrow to remember things you can give to God.

Prayer

God, thank You for loving me enough to do what You do as gifts for me. You are awesome! Amen.

God Never Changes

Jesus Christ is the same yesterday and today and forever.
– Hebrews 13:8

Teddy Bear

Do you have a favorite doll or teddy bear? Unlike God, favorite toys wear out. Put the teddy bear back together by drawing in what is missing.

Prayer

God, I am so glad You never change. I am thankful Your love never wears out and You never get tired of me. Amen.

God Never Changes

Jesus Christ is the same yesterday and today and forever.
– Hebrews 13:8

Satisfaction Jugs

In Jug A, draw toys you like. Then draw an "X" over Jug A, because toys wear out or get broken. Draw a heart shape in Jug B. Draw a circle around Jug B, because God's love never wears out. It is forever!

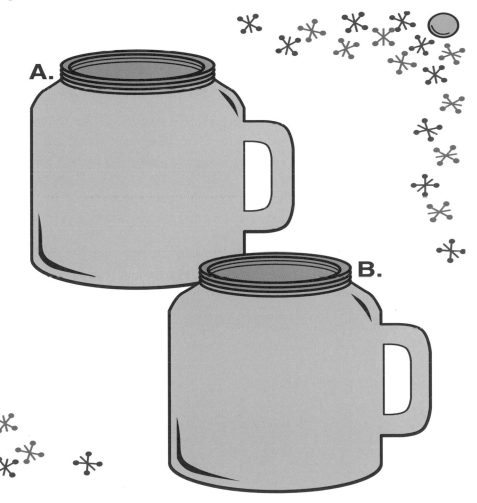

Prayer

Dear God, Thank You that You love me forever. Your love is the best gift! Amen.

God Enjoys Being with You

Be still, and know that I am God.
– Psalm 46:10

Quiet Places

"Be quiet!"

"Shh! Stop talking. I can't hear the TV."

"I am trying to sleep, so leave me alone."

Noise is everywhere. Do you have a quiet place of your own? Is it under your bed? In a closet? What about in a tree house? Maybe you have to get into the doghouse for peace and quiet. Is there anywhere you can go and not hear noise?

Jesus looked for quiet places too. He needed to get away from the noise and crowds so He could talk to God. One time He found a quiet place. It wasn't a tree house. It wasn't a closet. It wasn't even a bedroom. The place was a garden.

The garden was outside the walls that surrounded the city of Jerusalem. Jesus went there to pray and be alone with God. Jesus knew God wanted to talk with Him alone. God is with you when it is noisy. He is there when the TV is on. He is there when the radio is loud. But He likes being with you at quiet times too. God can speak to you anytime. But it can be easier to listen to Him when you are in a quiet place.

Your Turn

1. Do you have quiet places at your house? Where?
2. With your parents' permission, plan a time when you can meet with God in a quiet place. Then do it.

_____

_____

_____

Prayer

God, show me quiet places where I can meet with You each day. Amen.

God Enjoys Being with You

Be still, and know that I am God.
– Psalm 46:10

Quiet and Loud Places

Pretend the house is yours. Think of inside and outside quiet places at your home. Can you talk to God there? Draw a smiley face in each place in the house or outside where you can meet quietly with God to pray.

Prayer

Dear God, I want to meet with You every day. Please show me the best place to spend quiet time with You. Thank You. Amen.

God Enjoys Being with You

Be still, and know that I am God.
– Psalm 46:10

The Burning Bush

Draw a picture of what you think the burning bush looked like. Tonight, tell your family about the burning bush and ask them to pray with you. Take off your shoes and kneel to *Jehovah* (to God), like Moses did. Afterward, write down how you felt.

Prayer

Dear God, I know You are holy. I want to follow You all my life. Amen.

God Enjoys Being with You

Be still, and know that I am God.
– Psalm 46:10

Favorite First Photos

Do you know God is always with you? He was with you the first time you rode a bike. He was there the first time you fell and got hurt. He was there the first time you did well at school. Draw one of your favorite firsts and remember that God was with you.

Prayer

Thank You, God, for caring for me. I am so glad You are always with me. Amen.

God Enjoys Being with You

Be still, and know that I am God.
– Psalm 46:10

My Journal Page

Use this journal page to write to God. Tell Him about you and your friends and family. Share your feelings.

Prayer

Thank You, God, that I can call to You and You hear me and answer. Amen.

God Watches over You

*The L*ORD *is my shepherd, I lack nothing.*
– Psalm 23:1

The Good Shepherd

"It's time to turn the lights out. Go to sleep, Ruthie," Mother said.

"I can't go to sleep, Mom," Ruthie replied. "I'm worried about my speech at the contest at school tomorrow."

"I'd feel nervous too, Ruthie. Don't worry—you're ready. Besides, God, the good Shepherd, will be at the contest with you."

"The Shepherd? I thought shepherds just took care of sheep."

"That is right, Ruthie." Mother rubbed her back. "God is like a shepherd. He cares for you. He wants to help you in everything you do. You are like a little lamb to Him when you let Him care for your needs."

"Tell me more about the Shepherd and His sheep, Mom," Ruthie said through a yawn.

"We'll talk about sheep some more tomorrow night. Right now you need to get to sleep."

"Okay, you're right. Good night."

Your Turn

1. What are you worried about?
2. What helps you remember you belong to God?
3. What are ways God is like a shepherd? Thank Him for His care.

_____

_____

_____

_____

Prayer

God, I want to be Your lamb. Teach me to stay close to You. Amen.

God Watches over You

The LORD is my shepherd, I lack nothing.

– Psalm 23:1

Find the Shepherd

Draw a line to guide the lamb to the shepherd. Color the pictures.

Prayer

Thank You, God, for being my Shepherd and taking care of me. Help me never wander away from You. Amen.

God Watches over You

The LORD is my shepherd, I lack nothing.

– Psalm 23:1

911

When you are alone and scared, do you know what to do? You use the phone and call 911. The emergency operator will help you. Read Psalm 23. Find the verse in Psalm 23 that tells you not to fear because God is with you. Write it on the phone to remind you that God will give you peace and strength.

Prayer

Thank You, God, for being here. I am so glad You love me and watch over me day and night. Amen.

God Watches over You

The LORD is my shepherd, I lack nothing.

– Psalm 23:1

The Good Shepherd's Sheep

"Sheep with a loving shepherd don't worry about what will happen to them," Mother told Ruthie. "Do you know sheep are easily scared? They also don't sleep well if they're hungry. They get irritated by pesky flies that won't leave them alone. A good shepherd makes sure his flock is safe from wild animals. He makes sure his sheep have lots of green grass to eat. A good shepherd rubs special oil on the noses of his sheep to help keep flies away."

"It makes my nose itch just hearing about it," Ruthie said. "Can God be my good Shepherd?"

"Absolutely! God is your Shepherd!" Mother replied. "He will help you when you are worried and afraid. Let's pray to your good Shepherd right now and ask Him to give you His peace." Mother held Ruthie's hand and they prayed together.

Your Turn

1. How will God help you when you are worried?
2. What makes it easier to remember to ask God for help?

_____

_____

_____

_____

_____

Prayer

God, I am worried about _____.

Will You help me? Thank You for being my Shepherd. Amen.

God Watches over You

The LORD is my shepherd, I lack nothing.
– Psalm 23:1

Sheep's Pen Chart

Read Psalm 23 again. List three things you learned about God as your Shepherd.

_____

_____

_____

Prayer

God, I am so glad You are my good Shepherd. I don't have to be fearful because You are with me. Amen.

God Watches over You

The LORD is my shepherd, I lack nothing.

– Psalm 23:1

God Speaks

Make a recording of your voice and listen to it. Does your voice sound different than you thought it would? Draw a picture in each square of when God has spoken to you in your mind, in your heart, and through the Bible. If you did not listen and obey, tell Him you are sorry and ask Him to help you do better next time.

God spoke to me in my **mind**.

God spoke to me in my **heart**.

When God speaks, I should listen.

God spoke to me in the **Bible**.

Prayer

God, I know You love me and want to speak to me. I will be a good listener! Amen.

God Watches over You

The Lord is my shepherd, I lack nothing.
— Psalm 23:1

Discovering New Friends

Draw a picture of yourself inside the heart. Just as a shepherd loves his sheep, God loves you. Are there people you can know better? In the box, list people in your school or church you don't know very well. After asking your parents, invite each one to your house. Play a game called "Ten Questions." Take turns asking each other questions so you can learn about each other.

Prayer

I am glad I know You, God. Help me get to know the kids around me and show them Your love. Amen.

God Is Your Heavenly Father

Give thanks to the LORD, for he is good; his love endures forever.
– Psalm 106:1

A Happy Father

Have you ever been sick and stayed home from school? Have you been in a hospital? Your parents worry about you when you are sick.

In the Bible there is a story of a little girl who was very sick. Her father was named Jairus. He was an important man. He went to Jesus and bowed down. The man said, "My little girl is very sick. Please make her well."

Jesus loved the little girl and her father. He stopped what He was doing and went with the father. On the way, friends came and told Jairus that his daughter had died.

Jairus cried. Jesus said to him, "Don't be afraid; just believe." He went inside the house and told the sad people, "The child is not dead but asleep." He asked the people to leave. Jesus took the girl's hand and said, "Little girl, I say to you, get up." At once she stood up!

Her father and mother were happy and surprised. Jesus told them to give their daughter something to eat.

Your Turn

1. Do you think God was a happy heavenly Father when the girl was healed?
2. How does your Father in heaven feel when you are sick or have a problem?
3. Will you ask your earthly father and mother to pray for you when you are sick?

_____

_____

_____

Prayer

Thank You, God, for being my heavenly Father and loving me completely. Amen.

God Is Your Heavenly Father

Give thanks to the LORD, for he is good; his love endures forever.
– Psalm 106:1

My Father's Footprints

Color the footprints from your house all the way to God's house in heaven.

Prayer

Thank You, Father, for loving me. I know I can always count on You to listen and to care. Amen.

God Is Your Heavenly Father

Give thanks to the LORD, for he is good; his love endures forever.
– Psalm 106:1

Father's Gift

"Abba" means "Father" in the language Jesus spoke. Write "Abba" on one side of the bow and your name on the other side. Draw a picture of yourself in the center of the bow. Color the bow in your favorite color to remind you that God's love is the best gift ever!

Prayer

Abba, my God, I love You. You are my heavenly Father. I want to be close to You every day. Amen.

God Is Your Heavenly Father

Give thanks to the LORD, for he is good; his love endures forever.
– Psalm 106:1

Heaven Is a Beautiful Place

John was one of Jesus' disciples. God showed John what heaven is like. John wrote down what he saw. You can read it all in the book of Revelation, chapters 21 and 22.

John reported that heaven is beautiful. There is no sickness, no sadness and no tears! It is never dark there. God and Jesus are heaven's lights! There is no need for the sun or the moon. The gates to this beautiful city are made of pearl. They are always open. The streets are made of gold!

A river flows from God's throne, through the middle of the city. Beside the river grow trees that bear twelve kinds of fruit. In heaven, God's people see God face-to-face.

You can tell your friends about heaven. It is the place we all want to go!

Your Turn

1. Why do you think God showed His home to John?
2. Why do you think God and Jesus light up heaven?
3. Would you like to be with God in heaven someday?

_____

_____

_____

_____

_____

Prayer

Thank You, God, for telling John about Your home so he could tell me. I like knowing where Your house is. Amen.

God Is Your Heavenly Father

Give thanks to the LORD, for he is good; his love endures forever.
– Psalm 106:1

Streets of Gold

Revelation 21:21 says of heaven that "the great street of the city was of gold, as pure as transparent glass." Color the street of gold to the throne of God. Draw your face on the girl.

Prayer

God, I look forward to spending eternity in heaven with You someday. Amen.

God Is Your Heavenly Father

Give thanks to the LORD, for he is good; his love endures forever.
– Psalm 106:1

God's Home

Draw a picture showing what you think your place in heaven will look like.

Prayer

Thank You, Jesus, for preparing a special place for me in heaven. Amen.

God Is Your Heavenly Father

Give thanks to the LORD, for he is good; his love endures forever.
– Psalm 106:1

Treasure Chest

Heaven is a perfect place. The very best and happiest things are there! There is peace, happiness, and joy in God's heaven. It will be our home someday if we belong to Jesus. heavenly home. Draw pictures of the things you will be glad to see in heaven.

Prayer

Thank You, God, for heaven. I praise You and thank You for being my God and loving me. Amen.

God Wants You to Follow Him

*Obey the LORD your God and
carefully follow all his commands.*

– Deuteronomy 28:1

Rules, Rules, Rules

Kate listened carefully as Mrs. Green gave the classroom rules. *Every year I hear the same rules,* Kate thought.

"Rules are important," said Mrs. Green. "When riding your bike, one rule is to signal all turns with your hand. Table rules include using a spoon and fork. One classroom rule is to raise your hand before talking. At the swimming pool, one rule is not to dive in the shallow end. Rules are put in your path for a reason. Most rules help you be safe and keep others safe. Some are created to make life easier."

Kate knew Mrs. Green was right. Rules need to be in place to help people.

God gives you special rules. His rules keep you safe and show you when you are doing wrong in God's eyes. Doing wrong in God's eyes is called sin. Some of God's rules are called the Ten Commandments. They are listed in the Old Testament of the Bible, in Exodus 20. Do you know them? Look them up and read them out loud.

Your Turn

1. What are some rules you follow at home?
2. Why do your parents have rules for you?
3. Why would God want you to follow rules?

_____

_____

_____

Prayer

Thank You, God, for loving me enough to give me rules. I know You want to protect me from sin. You are a great God! Amen.

God Wants You to Follow Him

*Obey the L*ORD *your God and
carefully follow all his commands.*

– Deuteronomy 28:1

Rules to Follow

Think of rules your parents and God want you to follow. Now write your own rules to follow. For example, one rule might be to tell your parents thank you when they do something nice for you. Tell your parents about your rules so they can help you follow them.

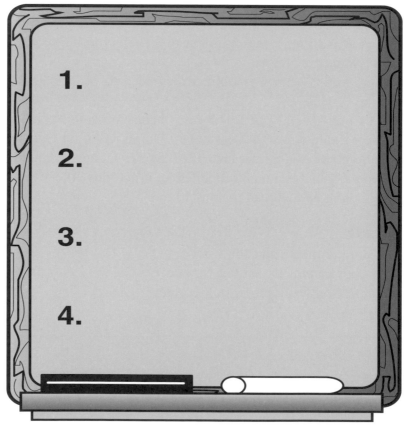

1.

2.

3.

4.

Prayer

God, I know Your rules are for my good, so please help me follow them. Amen.

God Wants You to Follow Him

Obey the LORD your God and
carefully follow all his commands.

– Deuteronomy 28:1

God, My King

God wants to be your King in every area of your life. Draw crowns on the heads that show how you should live if God is your King.

Prayer

God, You are the King of everything. Help me follow Your commands. You are my God, and I give You thanks. Amen.

53

God Wants You to Follow Him

*Obey the LORD your God and
carefully follow all his commands.*

– Deuteronomy 28:1

Pleasing God

"I hope she likes this card," said Cindy with a smile. Her class wanted to surprise their teacher with handmade birthday cards. Cindy really wanted to please Mrs. Carroll. She was Cindy's favorite teacher.

"It's okay to want to please your teachers, Cindy," said Dad. "When you please your teachers and parents, you please God too."

You want to please God. Always look for ways to do that. God and you make a wonderful team. Do your hands know what is pleasing to God? Do your feet? Do your eyes and mouth? Learning new things in school isn't always easy. Learning what pleases God isn't always easy, either. One place to start is by learning the Ten Commandments in the Bible. They are…

- Put God first.
- Love God most.
- Honor God's name.
- Make Sabbath days special.
- Honor your father and mother.
- Respect and protect life.
- Be true when you marry.
- Keep only what is yours.
- Be honest.
- Want only what is yours.

You obey and please God by following each one.

Your Turn

1. What is a reason to obey God's rules?
2. Choose one of the Ten Commandments. How will you obey it today?

_____

_____

_____

Prayer

Dear God, help me remember ways to please You and then do those things. Amen.

54

God Wants You to Follow Him

*Obey the L*ord *your God and carefully follow all his commands.*

– Deuteronomy 28:1

Living for God

Color the girl and think of ways to please God with your hands, feet, heart, lips, eyes, and ears. Write your ideas by the different body parts to help you remember.

Prayer

Lord, I want to discover how to please You. Help me read my Bible every day and talk to You. Amen.

God Wants You to Follow Him

Obey the LORD your God and carefully follow all his commands.

– Deuteronomy 28:1

God First

God's first rule is to *put Him first.* Nothing and no one is more important than God. Use the pictures to figure out the words for the crossword puzzle. The words in the puzzle are things that might take your attention away from God if you aren't careful.

Prayer

Dear LORD, help me always put You first. Amen.

God Wants You to Follow Him

Obey the LORD your God and carefully follow all his commands.

– Deuteronomy 28:1

Secret Messages

Use the heart dial to decode this secret message about loving God.

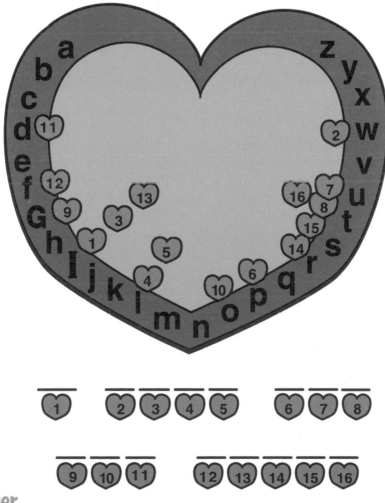

Prayer

I am glad You are my God. Please forgive me for not always putting You first. Amen.

Honoring God

*Love the LORD your God with all your heart and
with all your soul and with all your mind.*

– Matthew 22:37

Honor God's Name

Lazy-Lucy. Boy-Joy. Dopey-Hopey. Daffy-Kathy. Dianna-Banana. These are all examples of making fun of people by misusing their names. Has your name ever been turned into a bad or silly name? Sometimes people misuse names for no reason. How do you feel when people use your name to tease you?

"Sweet Lucy, I love you!" How do you feel when your name is used in a loving way like that?

How should God's name be used? Some people use His name and Jesus' name in anger or to try to sound tough or to be popular. Using God's name in the wrong way is a sin and makes God sad. There is never a good reason to misuse God's name.

When and how should you use God's name? God loves His name to be used to tell people about Jesus and Him. He loves to hear His name mentioned when you are thankful. Always protect and honor His name.

Your Turn

1. What are some times when people misuse God's name?
2. How can you use the name of God in good ways?

_____

_____

_____

_____

Prayer

Dear God, thank You for sharing Your powerful name with me. Your name is special, and I want to always use it in good ways. Amen.

Honoring God

*Love the L*ORD *your God with all your heart and
with all your soul and with all your mind.*

– Matthew 22:37

God's Name Tags

On each name tag, write another name you know for God. For example,
you might write "Loving Lord" or "King of kings." What's a way you can
show Him you love and honor His name today?

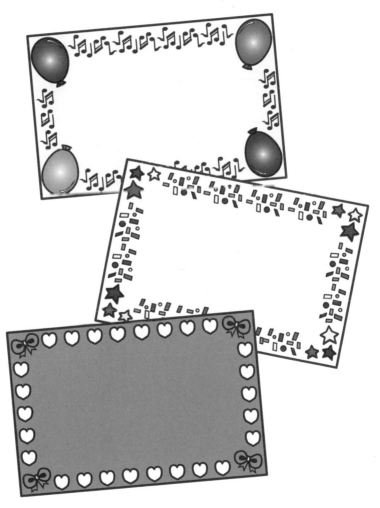

Prayer

Heavenly Father, I love You with all my heart and want to always honor
Your name. Amen.

59

Honoring God

Love the Lord *your God with all your heart and
with all your soul and with all your mind.*

– Matthew 22:37

Sabbath Dolls

Sabbaths are special days set aside to honor God. For Jewish people, the
Sabbath is celebrated on Saturday. Many Christians make Sunday their
special time of worship. Read Matthew 12:9-13 to find out some things
Jesus did on the Sabbath. Write on one doll what Jesus did that day. On
the other dolls, write your own ideas of good things you can do on the
Sabbath. When you are finished writing, color the dolls.

Prayer

God, help me to keep the Sabbath—Your day—special. I want to do
good things like You did. Amen.

Honoring God

*Love the LORD your God with all your heart and
with all your soul and with all your mind.*

– Matthew 22:37

Honoring Your Father and Mother

"Jessie, you promised to empty the trash and pick up your toys. Grandmother tripped over one of your dolls. She could fall and get hurt," said Mom.

God's Word says "honor your father and mother." That means He wants you to listen, obey, and love your parents. Honoring your parents encourages them and pleases God.

How can you honor your parents? Jessie had promised to pick up her toys. Jessie didn't keep her promise. Her grandmother could have been hurt because she didn't do what she said she would.

When you forget to honor your parents, it hurts you and others. What can you do to keep from making the same mistake Jessie did?

Your Turn

1. Why do you think God wants you to obey your parents?
2. Think of a time you obeyed. How did you feel? How did your parents feel?
3. What's a way you can obey today?

_____

_____

_____

_____

Prayer

Dear God, forgive me for the times when I didn't obey my parents. Help me keep my promises and honor my parents. Amen.

Honoring God

*Love the L*ORD *your God with all your heart and
with all your soul and with all your mind.*

– Matthew 22:37

The Promise Card

Will you promise God you will honor your parents? Fill out the Promise
Card. Also, write a note to your parents on a different sheet of paper. Tell
them how you plan to honor and obey them.

I, _____,

promise to honor

my parents by

loving them

and obeying them.

Prayer

Dear God, I know the rules You have for me are because You want the
best for me always. Please help me cheerfully obey my parents because
I know that pleases You. Amen.

Honoring God

*Love the L*ORD *your God with all your heart and
with all your soul and with all your mind.*

– Matthew 22:37

Teamwork

Draw a picture of yourself as part of the team. Remember, God wants
your family, your friends, and you to be on the same team—His team.

Prayer

God, please help me be true to my family and friends. Help me pick
friends who love You. Amen.

Honoring God

*Love the L*ORD *your God with all your heart and
with all your soul and with all your mind.*

– Matthew 22:37

Clean Hands

One of God's commandments is to not steal. To remind you to keep your hands clean and not steal, draw your arms and hands being washed in the sink. Write "I will not steal" on the clean towel.

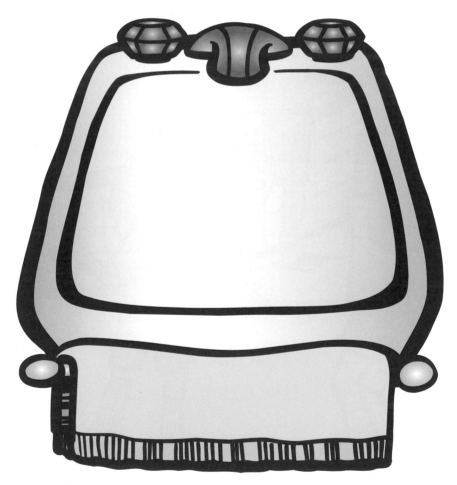

Prayer

God, I am thankful for Your lovingkindness. Teach me Your ways. Remind me not to steal. Amen.

Showing God's Love

*Clothe yourselves with compassion, kindness,
humility, gentleness and patience.*

– Colossians 3:12

Abigail's Kindness

Have you met someone who had pretty hair, nice eyes, and the best clothes? Her clothes were clean and stylish and included matching hair bows and shoes. Was she nice? Looking good on the outside doesn't mean a person is good on the inside.

David and his men were hiding from King Saul. Abigail and her husband, Nabal, lived nearby on a farm with goats and sheep (1 Samuel 25). David sent some soldiers to Nabal to ask for food because they had been protecting Nabal's shepherds and sheep. Nabal was rude and refused David's request. When Abigail heard about her husband's unkindness, she took action. She sent food and water to David and his men. She met David and asked him to be kind and ignore Nabal's rudeness.

Abigail knew how to clothe herself with kindness inside and out. After her husband died, she married David.

God cares about how you treat people. He wants you to treat others with kindness like Abigail treated David.

Your Turn

1. How can you show people you are beautiful on the inside?
2. What did you do the last time you were kind to someone?

_____

_____

_____

_____

Prayer

Dear LORD, show me how to be beautiful and kind on the outside and the inside. I want to treat people with kindness. Amen.

Showing God's Love

Clothe yourselves with compassion, kindness, humility, gentleness and patience.

– Colossians 3:12

Abigail's Kindness Key

The underlined words tell about Abigail's inner kindness and beauty. Look at the "Key" sentences. Write the underlined word next to the piece of clothing shown. When you're done, color the picture.

KEY

1. Abigail was <u>sweet</u>.

2. Abigail was <u>thoughtful</u>.

3. Abigail was <u>friendly</u>.

4. Abigail was <u>helpful</u>.

5. Abigail was <u>nice</u> with her words.

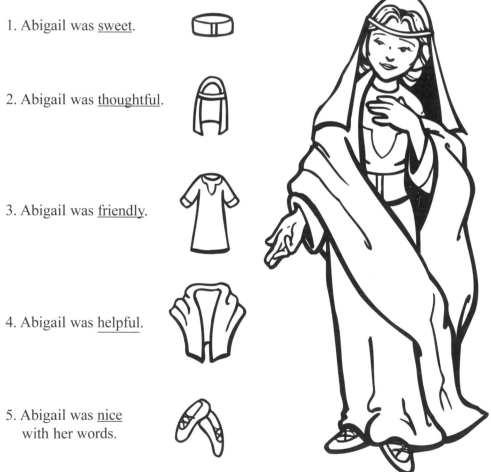

Prayer

Dear LORD, help me be sweet, thoughtful, friendly, and helpful. Amen.

Showing God's Love

*Clothe yourselves with compassion, kindness,
humility, gentleness and patience.*

– Colossians 3:12

The House of Kindness

God can help you use kind words in your house. In the house, draw a picture of how you can show kindness to your family. Write words of kindness in each room.

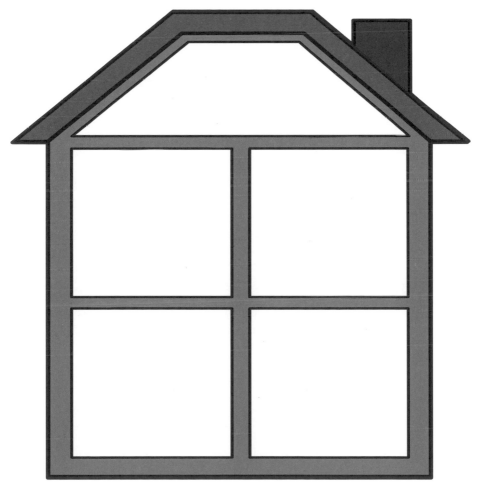

Prayer

Please forgive me, God, for my unkind words. Help me be friendlier and kinder. Amen.

67

Showing God's Love

Clothe yourselves with compassion, kindness,
humility, gentleness and patience.

– Colossians 3:12

Ruth Was Faithful

Do you have a best friend? The Bible says Naomi and her daughter-in-law Ruth were friends. They moved to Israel after their husbands died. Ruth could have gone to her hometown after her husband's death. Instead, she moved to Naomi's hometown in a different country. Ruth didn't want Naomi to be by herself so she made a special promise. Ruth said, "Where you go I will go, and where you stay I will stay. Your people will be my people and your God my God" (Ruth 1:16).

Ruth didn't have a job to make money to buy food. Instead, she went into the fields. "I'll pick up leftover grain," she said. Ruth was surprised when Boaz, the owner of the field, spoke to her.

"Your husband died," he said. "You left your father and mother and your homeland and came to live with a people you did not know before. May the LORD repay you for what you have done. May you be richly rewarded by the LORD, the God of Israel, under whose wings you have come to take refuge."

Your Turn

1. Who is a friend you have who sticks with you, like Ruth did?
2. When is it hard to stick with a friend? What makes it easier?

_____

_____

_____

Prayer

Thank You, LORD, for being my Friend. Show me how to be faithful to You and to my family. Amen.

Showing God's Love

*Clothe yourselves with compassion, kindness,
humility, gentleness and patience.*

– Colossians 3:12

My Promise Scroll

Ruth made a special promise to be faithful to Naomi. She didn't write her promise on a scroll, but you can. Fill in the promise scroll by writing down the name of a person you want to stay close to for a long time. Write how you will be her or his friend and what that means. For instance, "You, Karen, are my friend. I will always be kind and be truthful with you."

Prayer

Dear LORD, help me be faithful and loyal to my family and friends. And most of all, LORD, help me be faithful to You. Amen.

Showing God's Love

Clothe yourselves with compassion, kindness, humility, gentleness and patience.

– Colossians 3:12

Faithful Blackout

How can you show you're faithful to God? Black out with a dark crayon the pictures on the quilt that *do not* show faithfulness to God. Use a light-colored crayon to color the pictures that do show faithfulness to God.

Prayer

God, help me be loyal to people I know and love. Thank You for being faithful to me. Amen.

Showing God's Love

Clothe yourselves with compassion, kindness,
humility, gentleness and patience.

– Colossians 3:12

A Countable Heart

Ruth had a faithful, servant heart. She could be counted on for help and wise words. Do you have a faithful heart? Can you be counted on? What can your friends and family depend on from you? Copy the heart and color it and fill it out. Give it to a friend or family member you want to encourage.

_____ can count on

_____

(your name)

for _____ .

Prayer

Dear God, I know I can count on you. Show me how I can be a person people can depend on. Amen..

You Can Depend on God

We know and rely on the love God has for us.
– 1 John 4:16

God Is Trustworthy

"Hello, Kim? This is Keisha. Want to come over? We can practice our three-legged race for track day at school."

"Sure," Kim said.

Keisha asked, "Will you listen to me recite my poem for the contest too?"

"Yes!" replied Kim. "You can count on me."

"I know I can always count on you!" said Keisha.

Keisha knows her friend Kim will be there when she needs help. She also knows Kim will do what she says she will do. God is like that! He does what He says He will do. He says He will forgive you when you ask, and He always will. He says He will hear your prayers and answer the way He thinks best. And He does! You can count on God to always be here for you.

Your Turn

1. Who counts on you?
2. How can you show friends you are dependable?
3. How can you show God you depend on Him?

_____

_____

_____

_____

Prayer

God, I want people to count on me. Show me how I can show them I am dependable. Amen.

You Can Depend on God

We know and rely on the love God has for us.

– 1 John 4:16

Three-Legged Race

Put an X on the sack of the team you think is Keisha and Kim. Draw a line along the path until you get to the finish line. Win the three-legged race as a reminder that you can be counted on to show up and do what is right.

Prayer

God, please help me be the kind of girl my family and friends can count on. Amen.

You Can Depend on God

We know and rely on the love God has for us.

– 1 John 4:16

Right Paths

Color the pictures at the end of each road. Circle the lettered signs beside ways to please God. Draw a line from "Start" to the best place to finish.

Prayer

Please, God, teach me Your way. Lead me down good paths so I can lead others to You. Amen.

You Can Depend on God

We know and rely on the love God has for us.
– 1 John 4:16

Being a Leader for God

When you think of a courtroom, you probably think of a judge. The judge sits in the front behind a big desk called a bench. Before God gave Israel a king, the Israelites were ruled by judges. They ruled the land in times of peace and war.

There was a wise woman named Deborah who was a judge. People would come to her with their problems and arguments. Her courtroom was under a tree. Deborah is the only Israelite woman judge mentioned in the Bible. She was a great leader who listened to God.

The name "Deborah" means "bee." Deborah was busy as a bee helping the people of Israel. She even led the Israelites to war. God told Deborah what to do and Deborah told the general in charge of the army. God helped the Israelites win a battle against a scary enemy.

Deborah and the general, Barak, sang a special song of praise to God after the successful battle. Deborah loved God and wanted to be a good judge for Him. Are you a leader for God?

Your Turn

1. What are you good at?
2. What do you enjoy doing?
3. How can you use those things to honor God and lead for Him?

_____

_____

_____

Prayer

Thank You, God, for being my Leader. Help me be a leader for You. Teach me Your wisdom. Amen.

You Can Depend on God

We know and rely on the love God has for us.

– 1 John 4:16

Your Palm Tree

Deborah, a judge of Israel, under her own palm tree and listened to what the Israelites needed. They came to her to find answers and get help. She was the Israelite leader. Deborah loved God, and served Him by serving His people. How can you be a leader in your school and at home? Name your palm tree and draw yourself under it. God wants you to be a leader for Him.

Prayer

LORD, I want to be a leader for You in school, at church, and at home. Please help me listen to You and share Your wisdom. Amen.

You Can Depend on God

We know and rely on the love God has for us.
– 1 John 4:16

Queen Esther's Code

Esther was a very brave Jewish woman who became a queen. (You can read her fascinating story in the book of Esther in your Bible.) She counted on God's help, and God helped her to follow Him to save His people.

Use the code on Esther's crown to reveal Esther's message to you. Write each letter that goes with the number on the line. Can you solve the puzzle?

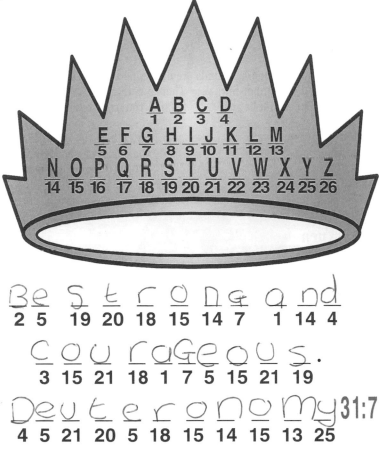

Be strong and
2 5   19 20 18 15 14 7   1 14 4

courageous.
3 15 21 18 1 7 5 15 21 19

Deuteronomy 31:7
4 5 21 20 5 18 15 14 15 13 25

Prayer

Dear God, I trust You to help me depend on You and do what You tell me to do. Give me a brave heart. Amen.

You Can Depend on God

We know and rely on the love God has for us.
– 1 John 4:16

Shadow Prayers

Do you ever get scared in the dark, or at night, or when the moon or other lights cause shadows to dance on your bedroom windows and walls? It's easy to get scared, but God wants you to know you can depend on Him to protect you and make your heart strong. When you get scared or nervous, ask God to give you His peace and His wisdom.

Write "God will help me be brave!" inside the shadow. When you are scared or nervous, ask God to fill your heart with peace and strength.

Prayer

God, I want to be brave when I see shadows at night. I trust You to help me feel safe. Amen.

God's Listens to You

Live as children of light . . .
and find out what pleases the LORD.

– Ephesians 5:8,10

Choose God's Way

"No school lessons! Vacation is here!" said Tasha.

"There are always lessons to be learned, Sweetie," Dad said.

"Like what?" asked Tasha.

"I know a lesson that is easy to know about but hard to do," said Dad.

He got his Bible and looked up today's verse. "The Bible says we should find out what pleases God and live His way," he said.

"Is that the lesson?" asked Tasha.

"Yes!" answered Dad. "First, you need to learn what pleases God, and then you choose God's way. You please God when you choose to obey His rules. It pleases God when you choose to help others. It also pleases God when you put others first. What do you think, Tasha?"

"I already do those things, Dad," said Tasha.

"Yes, but this lesson never ends," Dad said. "What are some things your mouth can say that please God? How could your hands do things God's way? Where could your feet go to that pleases God? I am still learning those things! As we find out what pleases Him, we think of more and more ways to choose His way!"

"I see what you mean, Dad."

Your Turn

1. Why is it sometimes hard to choose God's way?
2. Write down three ways you will please God this week.

_____

_____

_____

Prayer

God, show me what it means to choose Your way, and then help me do it. Amen.

God Listens to You

Live as children of light . . .
and find out what pleases the LORD.

– Ephesians 5:8,10

Just Do It!

The last part of today's verse says to please God. Can you "just do it" and choose God's way? Use the pictures to know where to write these words: hands, feet, mouth, ears.

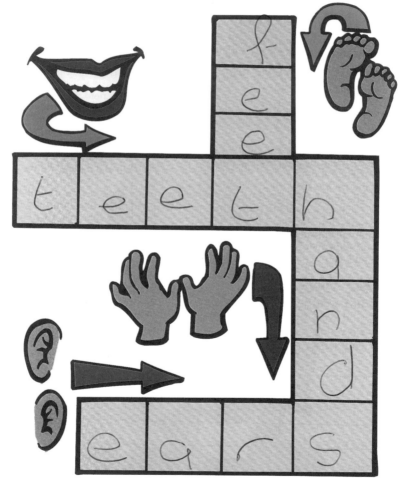

Prayer

God, help me know what it means to choose Your way. Help me follow You. Amen.

God Listens to You

Live as children of light . . .
and find out what pleases the LORD.

– Ephesians 5:8,10

A Woman of Prayer

Hannah prayed. She believed God always listened and always answered. She prayed for a long time that she would bear a child. God answered, and Hannah and her husband had a baby boy they named Samuel. (You can read more about Hannah in 1 Samuel 1.) Draw a line that follows the numbers around Hannah to put her inside God's house of prayer.

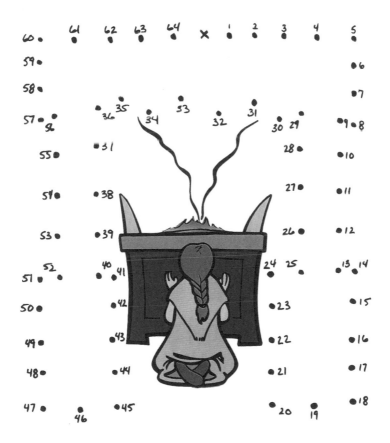

Prayer

Thank You, God, for listening to my prayers. I am glad You enjoy listening to me. Amen.

God Listens to You

Live as children of light . . .
and find out what pleases the LORD.

– Ephesians 5:8,10

You Can Pray

"How was school, Tina?" asked Dad at the dinner table.

"It was pretty good," answered Tina. "I found a great place to pray—the playground."

"On the playground?" Dad asked. "How can you pray there?"

"It's crowded, so no one notices when I pray," said Tina. "Plus, there's always something to pray for. Kids fall off the monkey bars and skin their knees playing ball. Today, I saw a boy hitting another boy. He got caught and had to sit out the rest of the recess. I prayed God would help him learn that hitting isn't the way to solve problems. Then later, while I was swinging, I thought of the Shanks. They are moving next month to be missionaries. I asked God to help my friend Anna adjust to life far from here."

Dad spoke up. "Prayer is good anywhere and anytime! Jesus said, 'When you pray, go into your room, close the door and pray to your Father, who is unseen.' You can pray anywhere and anytime!"

Tina's dad is right. If you pray inside your head and not out loud, you are praying in secret. Silent playground prayers are just as good as praying anywhere else.

Your Turn

1. Why did Jesus say to pray in secret?
2. Does it matter to God where or when you pray?
3. Can you think of a new place where you can pray?

_____

_____

_____

Prayer

God, thank You for letting me talk to You anytime and anywhere. Show me the people You want me to pray for. Amen.

God Listens to You

Live as children of light . . .
and find out what pleases the LORD.

– Ephesians 5:8,10

Playground Prayer

Write on the playground the names of people you know who need prayer.
Color the picture while you pray.

Prayer

Lord, I can pray anytime. Thank You for listening and answering. Amen.

God Listens to You

Live as children of light . . .
and find out what pleases the LORD.

– Ephesians 5:8,10

Good Works Fabric

Dorcas loved Jesus. She was always doing good and helping the poor. One of her good works was sewing clothes for people in need. Can you think of ways you can do good works by helping people?

Prayer

Teach me, dear God, to care about people. I want to be like Dorcas and help. Amen.

God Listens to You

Live as children of light . . .
and find out what pleases the LORD.

– Ephesians 5:8,10

How to Make a Decision

When you have to make a decision, one way to decide is to ask, "What would Jesus do?" Find and circle those four words in the puzzle. Each word might go down, across, or up.

Q R K W I J

S L M H M E

Z F P A Z S

W U O T O U

W O U L D S

Prayer

Dear God, help me remember to ask You what You want me to do. Remind me to ask, "What would Jesus do?" Amen.

Be Joyful

Is anyone happy? Let them sing songs of praise.
– James 5:13

A Happy Woman

Jesus told stories to teach people about His love. Here is one of them based on a story recorded in Luke 15.

There was a woman with ten silver coins. Back in ancient times, people worked many hours to earn just one coin. The woman lost one of them.

"Oh, no!" she said and sighed. "What did I do with that coin? I will have to clean the house and look in every cupboard and closet."

The woman looked for the coin. She turned over every piece of furniture. Suddenly, she found it! What a wonderful surprise! She was so happy she called all her friends and told them the good news. "I had ten silver coins, and I lost one. I was so sad and worried. I found the coin when I cleaned my house," she said. "I'm so happy. Please be happy with me."

Proverbs 15:13 says, "A happy heart makes the face cheerful." The woman had a cheerful face when she found her coin.

Your Turn

1. Do you share what makes you happy with others?
2. Do people know you are happy because you love Jesus?

_____

_____

_____

_____

Prayer

Thank You, Jesus, for loving me. Your love makes me happy. Amen.

Be Joyful

Is anyone happy? Let them sing songs of praise.
– James 5:13

The Coin

Inside the coin, write the names of friends you know who need to hear about Jesus. What are some ways you can share the good news of Jesus with them?

Prayer

God, knowing You fills me with joy! Help me share the good news of knowing You with my friends. Amen.

Be Joyful

Is anyone happy? Let them sing songs of praise.
– James 5:13

My Measuring Cup

God love us. He gives us everything we need to be filled with joy. Beside the cup, list four things next that give you joy. It is like God's good recipe for you life! Color the cup to the full line to show how much joy God gives you.

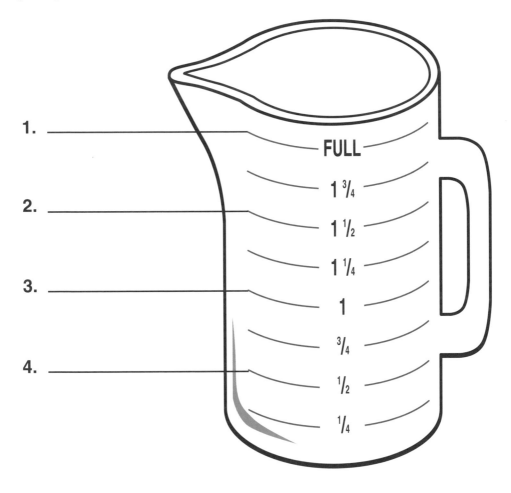

1.
2.
3.
4.

Prayer

Thank You, God, for loving me and providing just what I need to be happy in You. Amen.

Be Joyful

Is anyone happy? Let them sing songs of praise.
– James 5:13

You Can Be Happy

"Mother!" cried Amanda as she ran into the house.

"What is it, Amanda?" Mom asked quickly.

"Grumpy Mr. Ginn chased Abby and me out of his yard," Amanda answered. "He said his yard is a home for special birds, and we were scaring them away. We weren't doing anything wrong—just walking across his yard. He acts so grumpy, and he never smiles."

"Well, maybe you had better stay out of his yard," said Mom.

"Mom, do you think Mr. Ginn is happy inside?" Amanda asked. "He sure doesn't look happy outside."

"You can tell when people are happy inside because they usually smile. It's hard to say with Mr. Ginn because we don't see him every day. Only God knows what's in his heart for sure," said Mom. "The Bible tells us in Psalm 4:7 that David asked God to fill his heart with joy. Just knowing God loved him made David happy."

Mom hugged Amanda. "God loves us too. He loves us so much that He asked His only Son, Jesus, to die on a cross for our sins."

Amanda nodded. She thought, *Mr. Ginn doesn't seem to know how much God loves him.*

Your Turn

1. What makes you grumpy?
2. How can knowing God loves you help you smile?

_____

_____

_____

Prayer

Dear God, help me remember that You love me, so I can be happy on the inside and love others. Amen.

Be Joyful

Is anyone happy? Let them sing songs of praise.
– James 5:13

Happy Faces

People have many kinds of faces! Below each face, write an "S" for sad, an "H" for happy or a "G" for grumpy. Then draw happy faces down the right side while you sing a song of praise to God.

Prayer

Dear God, knowing You makes me happy! Amen.

Be Joyful

Is anyone happy? Let them sing songs of praise.
– James 5:13

God and You

Decorate and color the friendship necklace. Write "God and Me" on the necklace to remind you that God is your best friend.

Prayer

Thank You, God, for being my friend. Teach me to be a good friend. Amen.

Be Joyful

Is anyone happy? Let them sing songs of praise.

– James 5:13

I Love You, God

Tell God you love Him using each finger of your hand. Trace around your hand. Then write one of the words in color on a finger. When you pray, remember to use the idea on each of your fingers. Why not pray them right now?

1. Thanks: Thank You for Your love to me.

2. Sing: You are a God worthy of loving.

3. Obey: I will read and obey the Bible because I love You.

4. Tell: I love You, God.

5. Pray: I pray that my friends will know Your love, God.

Prayer

Jesus, thank You for loving me. Knowing that You saved me makes my heart happy. Amen.

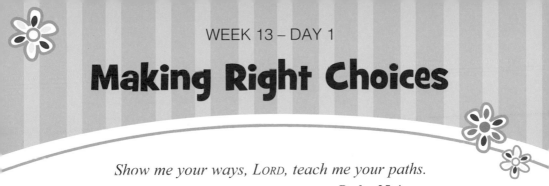

Making Right Choices

*Show me your ways, L*ORD*, teach me your paths.*
– Psalm 25:4

Lydia Chose God's Way

In Bible times, travelers asked anyone along the road for a place to sleep at night. People who loved God offered food and shelter for each other as they traveled from town to town.

A woman named Lydia was kind to everyone she met. Lydia owned her own business. She sold purple cloth and purple dye, which was hard to get. Purple was a desired color in Bible days, and Lydia became rich.

One day Lydia and her friends gathered at the river to pray to God. A man of God named Paul stopped at the river to tell the people about Jesus. Lydia hadn't heard about Him. She didn't know that He died for her sins so she could know God personally.

Lydia listened to Paul as he talked. She prayed too. That same day, Lydia and her family were baptized in the river! She wanted people to know she was happy to know Jesus. Lydia decided to live God's way through Jesus Christ. Lydia asked Paul and his friends to stay at her home. Lydia loved God and chose to do things His way.

Your Turn

1. How can you choose God's way through Jesus like Lydia did?
2. How can you be kind to people you meet?

_____

_____

_____

_____

Prayer

God, help me choose Your way in everything I do. I open my heart to Jesus. Amen.

Making Right Choices

Show me your ways, LORD, teach me your paths.
– Psalm 25:4

Adopt a Family

Lydia cared for other people. This is one way she showed she loved Jesus. With your parents, think of another family with children that your own family could help. You can "adopt" the children for Christmas and birthdays by buying gifts for them. If they need food, you can take groceries to them. To help you remember, fill out the adoption papers and begin helping others as Lydia did!

ADOPTION PAPERS

NAME OF FAMILY

ADDRESS

PHONE NUMBER

BIRTHDAYS

Prayer

Dear God, I know that one way to be happy is to help people. Please open my eyes to see anyone around me who needs help. Amen.

Making Right Choices

*Show me your ways, L*ORD*, teach me your paths.*
– Psalm 25:4

Bible Search

Psalm 119:103 says, "How sweet are your words to my taste, [LORD,] sweeter than honey to my mouth!" God's Word is sweet and powerful. On the honey bear, write words from the Bible—favorite verses from this book or verses you have memorized. They are some sweet words!

Prayer

Thank You, God, for Your sweet messages that tell me You love me. I am so happy to be Your child. Amen.

Making Right Choices

Show me your ways, LORD, teach me your paths.
– Psalm 25:4

Following God

Do you know the meaning of your name? Names have specific meanings. One lady in the Bible was named. "Sarah." It means "princess." Sarah learned to follow God. One day, Abraham told Sarah some special news. God had told him, "Go from your country...to the land I will show you" (Genesis 12:1).

Sarah listened as Abraham told her God's message. She could have asked, "What place is this? How long will we be there? What about leaving my family and friends?" But instead, she began packing!

They moved to the land of Canaan. God told Abraham, "To your offspring I will give this land." Sarah trusted God to guide Abraham, and Abraham trusted God to lead him.

God keeps His promises. He does what He says He will do. That is the reason you can trust Him, too!

Your Turn

1. How would you feel if your family had to move?
2. What is a way you can show God you love and follow Him?

_____

_____

_____

_____

Prayer

Dear God, I want to be a follower of You like Abraham and Sarah. Teach me to trust You as they did. Amen.

Making Right Choices

Show me your ways, LORD, teach me your paths.
– Psalm 25:4

Following God Bag

Following God meant Sarah moved from her home to a strange land. What do you do to follow God? What does He ask you to do? Write your ideas in Sarah's bag. Pray and ask God to help you do these things and follow Him faithfully.

Prayer

LORD, I want to trust You and follow the path You set for me. Amen.

Making Right Choices

Show me your ways, Lord, teach me your paths.
– Psalm 25:4

Dancing Shoes

Following God's way is like joining Him in a beautiful dance. On the dance shoes, write different ways you follow God at school, at home, and at church.

Prayer

God, help me follow You everywhere I go. Show me how to live Your way. Amen.

Making Right Choices

Show me your ways, LORD, teach me your paths.
– Psalm 25:4

Choose Me

Look up these words in a dictionary:

select   pick   favor   choose   want

Use these words to complete these sentences:

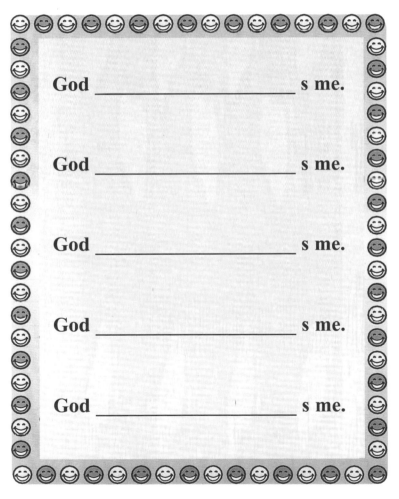

God _____ s me.

God _____ s me.

God _____ s me.

God _____ s me.

God _____ s me.

Prayer

Thank You, God, for choosing me as Your daughter. I am glad You did.
Amen.

Look to Jesus

My eyes are ever on the LORD.

–Psalm 25:15

Focus on Jesus

Missionaries are people who go around telling others about Jesus. Paul was a missionary in Bible times. He met a woman named Phoebe who loved Jesus. Phoebe helped many people, including Paul. She took a message from Paul to a church in a city called Rome. In the letter, Paul told the people to welcome Phoebe and provide anything she needed because she was a deacon in the church.

"Deacon" means "servant." Deacons help people at church in special ways. Phoebe may have provided food and a place for believers in Jesus to meet. She may have sewn clothes for people who needed them. The Bible doesn't tell us exactly what she did, but she did help many people.

Paul said good things about Phoebe and thanked her for her goodness.

Phoebe kept her eyes on Jesus. He helped her to love and care for the people around her.

What are some ways you can be like Phoebe? Ask Jesus to show you how you can help people.

Your Turn

1. Why do you think Phoebe helped people?
2. How do you know Phoebe kept her eyes on Jesus?
3. How can you keep your eyes on Jesus?

_____

_____

_____

Prayer

Dear God, teach me to help others. Let my eyes see people who need help. Amen.

Look to Jesus

My eyes are ever on the LORD.

–Psalm 25:15

Seeing Jesus

Across the top half of the page, write today's Bible verse. Then at the bottom of he page, draw a picture of your eyes looking up to the LORD. Remember to always look to Jesus for help so you know what to do.

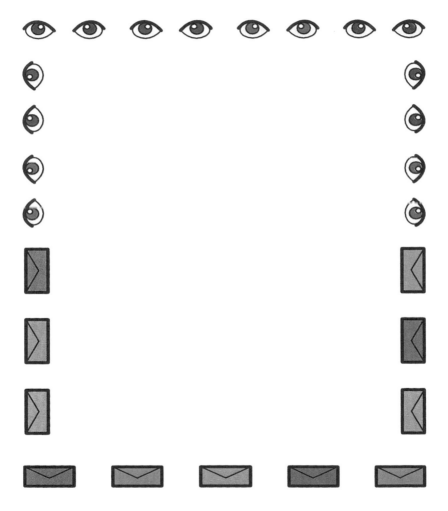

Prayer

Dear God, I want to keep my eyes focused on You because I know You will teach me how to live right. Amen.

Look to Jesus

*My eyes are ever on the L*ORD.

–Psalm 25:15

Bible Tracks

Use this page to track your Bible reading each day for two weeks. Color in the footprint each day you read your Bible. (You can copy this page to use over and over for a month or even a year.) You can also color a footprint if your parents read the Bible to you. Ask for help with new words. Write them down and what they mean on this page so you will remember. Happy reading!

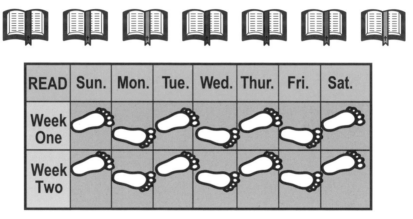

READ	Sun.	Mon.	Tue.	Wed.	Thur.	Fri.	Sat.
Week One							
Week Two							

_____

_____

_____

_____

_____

Prayer

Thank You, God, for giving me Your Word to read. Remind me to read it every day. Amen.

Look to Jesus

My eyes are ever on the LORD.
–Psalm 25:15

Thanking God

Miriam was the sister of Moses and Aaron. She loved to worship God. She was a leader of the Israelite women (Micah 6:4).

Once, God split the sea. Moses held his walking stick out toward the water. God made a wall of water and dried the land. The people of Israel took their goods and walked across the sea to the other side.

The Israelites were running from the mean Pharaoh of Egypt. He had set the people of Israel free from slavery, but then he changed his mind.

After God's people got to the other side of the sea, the sea rushed forward. The Pharaoh's soldiers and horses were killed.

When Miriam saw how God had helped them, she was very thankful. She took a small drum with bells and danced before the LORD. The women followed her as she sang a song of thanks to God: "Sing to the LORD for he is highly exalted. Both horse and driver he has hurled into the sea" (Exodus 15:21).

Your Turn

1. Name some things you want to thank God for.
2. What should you do when you are thankful to God?

_____

_____

_____

_____

Prayer

Thank You, LORD, for the times You have helped me. I will sing praises to You. Amen.

Look to Jesus

My eyes are ever on the LORD.

–Psalm 25:15

Music Puzzle

Miriam played a drum with bells on it when she sang and danced before God and the Israelite women. Read the letters on each bell tied to the drum. Place the letter that matches the number in the message to discover what you can sing to God.

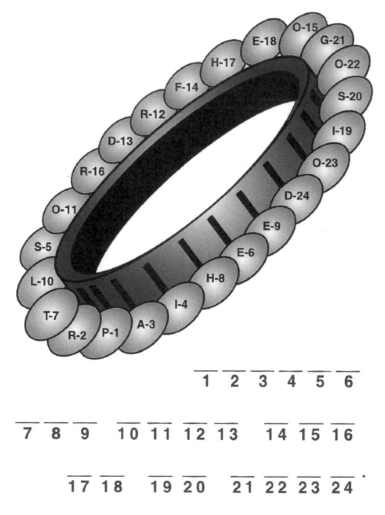

$$\overline{1}\ \overline{2}\ \overline{3}\ \overline{4}\ \overline{5}\ \overline{6}$$

$$\overline{7}\ \overline{8}\ \overline{9}\ \ \overline{10}\ \overline{11}\ \overline{12}\ \overline{13}\ \ \overline{14}\ \overline{15}\ \overline{16}$$

$$\overline{17}\ \overline{18}\ \ \overline{19}\ \overline{20}\ \ \overline{21}\ \overline{22}\ \overline{23}\ \overline{24}.$$

Prayer

LORD, You are so good to me! I want to sing and worship You. Amen.

Look to Jesus

My eyes are ever on the LORD.

–Psalm 25:15

An Important Message

This week you have been discovering how people trust Jesus to help them and guide them. Using the "Start" cross, follow the dots up and around. Say the words out loud to discover an important message. Do this three times so you will remember what to do every day.

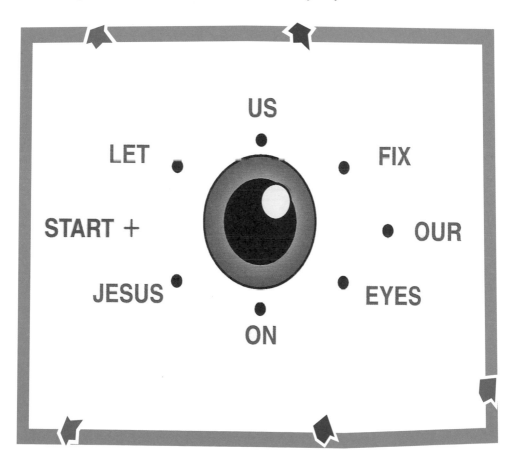

Prayer

Jesus, help me to keep my eyes on You so I can follow You without getting lost. Amen.

Look to Jesus

My eyes are ever on the LORD.

–Psalm 25:15

Goliath Hill

God wants you to thank Him for everything—whether it's something big like this big hill, or something little. He wants you to thank Him whether you get something you like or something you don't like. The Bible tells us to praise God in everything!

On this "giant" hill (named Goliath!), write some things that are hard for you to do. In the sky, write words to thank God for ways He has helped you.

Prayer

Thank You, God, for the love and care You give me every day. Amen.

106

Love Jesus!

You love [Jesus] even though you have never seen him.
– 1 Peter 1:8 TLB

Loving Someone You Can't See

Ella and her mother walked the hall at St. James Hospital looking for Grandpa's room. Ella stopped in the middle of the hall.

"Look at this picture of Jesus on the wall, Mom. Is this what Jesus really looked like?" Ella asked.

"Probably not, Ella," Mom answered. "Nobody really knows what Jesus looked like. There were no cameras that long ago."

"I'd like to see Jesus and know what He really looks like," said Ella.

"Would that make you love Him more, Ella?" asked Mom.

"No," answered Ella. "I love Him even though I can't see Him. It doesn't matter what He looks like. I love Him because I know what He did for me."

Mom took Ella's hand. "In the Bible, Jesus' friend Peter wrote to tell us that even when tough things happen, we should praise God. Peter also wrote hat even though we have never seen Jesus, we know we can trust Him. Ella, I am glad that you don't need to see Jesus in order to trust Him."

Your Turn

1. Jesus was born in the land called Israel. Find photos of people who live in Israel. What do you think Jesus looked like when he was a boy?
2. What is a way you can show Jesus you love and trust Him today?

_____

_____

_____

Prayer

I love You, Jesus, even though I can't see You. Amen.

Love Jesus!

You love [Jesus] even though you have never seen him.
– 1 Peter 1:8 TLB

A Heart Puzzle

Look at each picture. Write the first letter of the name of each thing on the blank above it. Read the message, and then draw something in each smaller heart that reminds you of what Jesus has done for you.

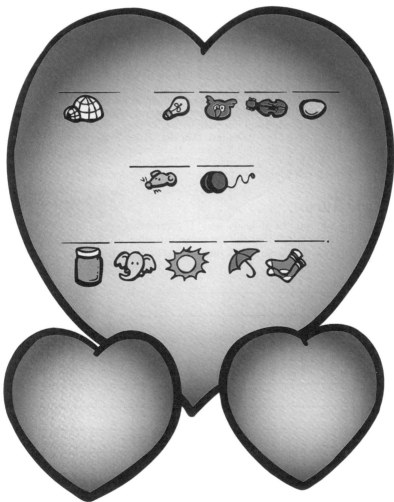

Prayer

LORD, I love You more than anyone and anything! Help me live according to Your plan. Amen.

Love Jesus!

You love [Jesus] even though you have never seen him.
– 1 Peter 1:8 TLB

Thank-You Card

Design a thank-You card to God. On the front, draw pictures of the things you do because you love Him.

Thank You, God

Prayer

Dear God, I love You. Thank You for loving me first, even before I knew You! Amen.

Love Jesus!

You love [Jesus] even though you have never seen him.
– 1 Peter 1:8 TLB

A Parent's Love

"I love you, Maddie," Mom said.

"I love you too, Mom," answered Maddie.

Maddie's mother smiled as she remembered holding and rocking Maddie when she was a baby. Mom had saved that memory in her heart. She loved Maddie and wanted to remember special times with her.

Jesus' mother loved her Son too. At Jesus' birth, she wrapped Him tightly in a warm blanket and laid Him in a manger. Mary saved the memory of that night in her heart.

When He was around twelve, Jesus and His family traveled to Jerusalem for a special Jewish celebration. When Joseph and Mary headed home, they suddenly noticed Jesus was not in the group they were traveling with. Filled with worry and love, Mary and her husband went back to Jerusalem. They finally found Him.

Jesus was sitting in the temple listening to the religious teachers and asking questions. Mary asked Him why He had caused her to worry so much. She was worried because she loved Him!

Mary was there when Jesus was born, and she was there when He was killed on the cross. Mary loved Jesus!

What are some happy things you remember about Jesus?

Your Turn

1. What memories of love do you keep in your heart?
2. What's a memory of Jesus that is special to you?

_____

_____

Prayer

Dear God, help me love Jesus more every day. Amen.

Love Jesus!

You love [Jesus] even though you have never seen him.
– 1 Peter 1:8 TLB

Your Heart Memories

What are some memories of love you keep in your heart? Draw a picture or list them in the heart. Let your heart memories remind you of the love Mary had for Jesus. Jesus wants your love too. Do you love Him?

Prayer

Jesus, I know that one way I show my love for You is by loving others. Please help me do that. Amen.

Love Jesus!

You love [Jesus] even though you have never seen him.
– 1 Peter 1:8 TLB

The Friendship Bracelet

Trace the dotted lines to create a friendship bracelet. Write your name on the line.

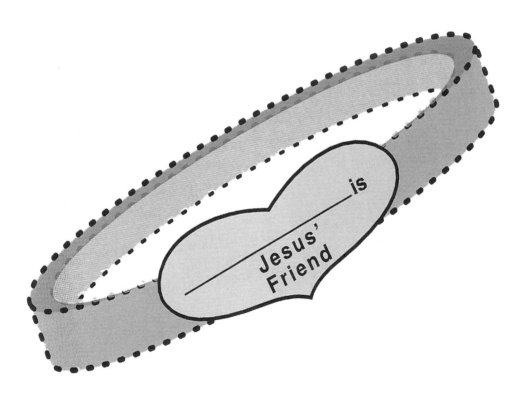

Prayer

Dear Jesus, I am so thankful that You are my friend. I love You! Amen.

Love Jesus!

You love [Jesus] even though you have never seen him.
– 1 Peter 1:8 TLB

Friendship Pages

On the friendship pages, write on the left side how you can love Jesus more and be a better friend.

Prayer

Dear Jesus, I want everyone to know that You are my best friend. Amen.

Blessing Jesus

Let all that I am praise the LORD.
–Psalm 103:1 NLT

With All that Is Within You

Rowing a boat is hard work. After boating for a while, you have to row harder and harder to get to shore, especially if the wind is blowing. You have to row with all your might…with all that is within you. Running a race is the same way. You want to win so you run with all that is within you to the finish line.

A woman named Joanna wanted to bless Jesus with all that was within her. She was thankful because Jesus had healed her (Luke 8:1-3). Joanna traveled with Jesus and His disciples. She used her own money to help buy food and other things Jesus and the disciples needed.

After Jesus died, Joanna bought spices and oils to prepare Jesus' body for burial. She was among the women who found Jesus' empty tomb. She was one of the women who told the disciples Jesus had risen.

With everything that was within Joanna, she blessed Jesus. When King David wrote today's Scripture verse, "Let all that I am praise the LORD," he meant, "I want to thank God with everything inside me." What do you think it looks like to bless Jesus with all that is in you?

Your Turn

1. Why did Joanna want to bless Jesus with all that was within her?
2. Do you have reasons to bless Jesus with all that is within you?
3. How can you show Jesus you want to bless His holy name?

_____

_____

_____

Prayer

Dear God, thank You for sending Jesus to die for me. Teach me how to bless You and Jesus with all that is within me. Amen.

Blessing Jesus

Let all that I am praise the LORD.
–Psalm 103:1 NLT

Row Your Boat

Jesus died on the cross so you could be saved and have a close, loving relationship with Him. That alone is a BIG reason to bless His holy name. What other reasons do you have to praise and thank Jesus? How will you bless (say good things about) Him? Write your ideas on the boat oars.

Prayer

Dear LORD, I love You and want to praise Your holy name with all that I am. Amen.

115

Blessing Jesus

Let all that I am praise the LORD.
–Psalm 103:1 NLT

Making Your Plan

On the pictures below, write the things you plan to do to bless Jesus.

Prayer

Dear God, thank You for being so willing to forgive me. I love You and Jesus and want to be a blessing for You. Help me love others so I can be a blessing to them. Amen.

116

Blessing Jesus

Let all that I am praise the LORD.
–Psalm 103:1 NLT

Showing Your Goodness

The Bible tells a terrific story about a brave woman named Rahab.

Joshua was the leader of the Israelites. They were going to take over the city of Jericho. Joshua sent two spies to check out the city.

Rahab lived in a house built on a city wall. The spies met Rahab, and when the soldiers tried to find them, she hid them on the roof.

The king's men searched her house but did not find the spies. Rahab told the soldiers the spies were long gone. When night came, she told the two men she had heard of the Israelites and their mighty God. She asked them to not hurt her family when they attacked. The men told her if she put a red cord in the window and gathered her family, they would be safe.

Rahab lowered a rope over the wall and told the men where to hide until it was safe. When the spies got back to Joshua, they told him about Rahab. Joshua told his troops to leave her house alone.

Rahab was brave and helped the Israelites. She was was rewarded by God. When the army came, Rahab and her family stayed safe.

Your Turn

1. Why do you think Rahab took a chance and hid the spies?
2. What did the spies promise?
3. What is something good you can do that might seem scary or hard at first?

_____

_____

_____

_____

Prayer

God, show me how to do good. I want to help people know You. Amen.

Blessing Jesus

Let all that I am praise the LORD.
–Psalm 103:1 NLT

Goodness Rope

The Bible says, "All who trust in God will devote themselves to doing good" (Titus 3:8 NLT). What does it really mean to do good? Look up the word "good" in a dictionary. On the lines by the rope, write the words from the dictionary that tell what it is to be and do good. For example, you might write "doing the right thing."

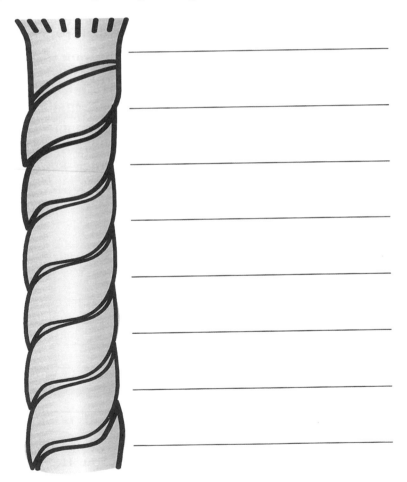

_____

_____

_____

_____

_____

_____

_____

Prayer

LORD, one way I praise you is by doing good to others and telling them about You. Amen.

118

Blessing Jesus

Let all that I am praise the LORD.
–Psalm 103:1 NLT

Headline Scramble

Jesus wants you to always do good to others. Figure out the headline for this news website. Match the happy faces and put the correct words on the lines. You'll discover a great message to you from God.

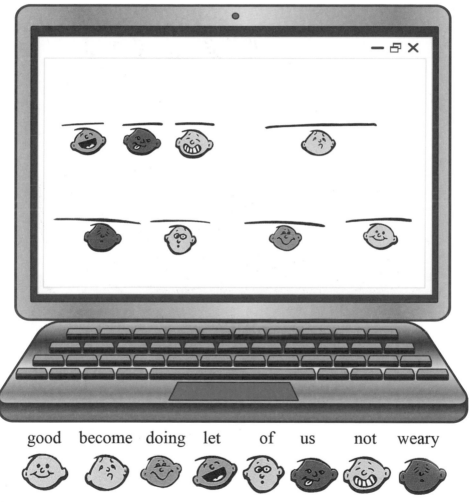

good become doing let of us not weary

Prayer

Dear Jesus, thank You for loving me enough to help me even when I don't do good. Help me to notice Your goodness and remember to praise Your name. Amen.

Blessing Jesus

Let all that I am praise the LORD.
–Psalm 103:1 NLT

Raindrop Scramble

Match the letters in the raindrops with the numbers below the lines to find an important message.

$\overline{}\ \overline{}\ \overline{}\quad \overline{}\ \overline{}\ \overline{}\ \overline{}$
1　 2　 3　　 4　 5　 6　 7

$\overline{}\ \overline{}\quad \overline{}\ \overline{}\ \overline{}\ \overline{}$.
8　 9　　 10　 11　 12　 13

Prayer

Dear God, I know You love me. You are a good God, and I trust You. Amen.

Doing What Is Right

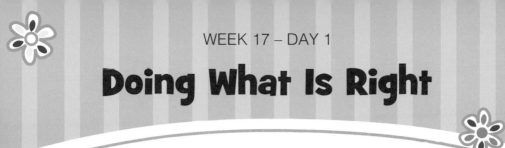

*Do what is right and good in the L*ORD*'s sight.*
– Deuteronomy 6:18

Doing the Right Thing

Helping other people is always the right thing to do. In the Bible (2 Kings 5) you can read about a young girl who bravely did the right thing. She was taken by the enemy in a war. She became a slave and served the wife of the army commander, named Naaman.

Naaman was an enemy of Israel, the country where the slave girl was from. Now, he had a terrible skin disease. The slave girl felt sorry for him.

She said to Naaman's wife, "I wish Naaman would go to God's prophet Elisha in Israel. He would heal him."

When Naaman heard this, he set off for Israel. But Elisha did not see him. Instead, he sent a message to Naaman: "Wash seven times in the Jordan River to be healed."

At first Naaman was angry. He was important and thought Elisha should have met him. Finally, he did what Elisha said—and God healed him!

Although forced to be a slave, the young girl did the right thing by telling Naaman's wife about Elisha. She did not want Naaman to suffer. She did the right thing and helped the family she served.

Your Turn

1. Why do you think the young girl helped Naaman?
2. Why is it sometimes hard to do the right thing?

_____

_____

_____

_____

Prayer

LORD, help me do the right thing even when it is hard. Amen.

Doing What Is Right

Do what is right and good in the LORD's sight.
– Deuteronomy 6:18

Word Puzzle

The young slave girl did what was right and pleased God. Fill in the missing letters below. Review the verse to fill in the blanks if you need to.

D____   w____a____   i____

r____g____t   __nd

____oo____   ____ ____

t____ ____   L____ ____ ____'s

s____g____t.

Deuteronomy 6:18

I'm glad I did the right thing.

Prayer

LORD, help me know what is right in Your sight and then do it. Amen.

Doing What Is Right

Do what is right and good in the LORD's sight.
– Deuteronomy 6:18

Checkers

Look at the checkerboard. Draw arrows to move your checker to the squares that tell you the right thing to do. The first one is done for you.

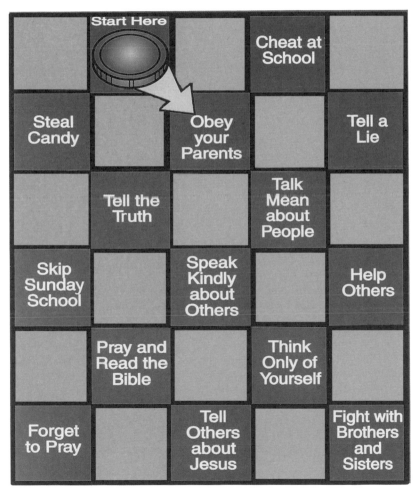

Prayer

Dear God, help me understand how to do right by following Your wisdom in the Bible. When I do wrong, please put me back on the right path. Amen.

Doing What Is Right

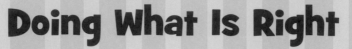

Do what is right and good in the LORD's sight.
– Deuteronomy 6:18

Sharing God's Word

Do you know who President Abraham Lincoln was? He went to school at home. He lived in the woods far from a school building. His mother taught him science, history, math, and the Bible. He loved learning.

Timothy, a follower of Jesus in Bible times. was also schooled at home. His mother, Eunice, and his grandmother Lois were his teachers. They taught him the ways of God and the Bible. The name "Timothy" means "one who honors God." Lois and Eunice taught him to honor God. Timothy helped the apostle Paul meet people and share Jesus' love for them and that He died for their sins.

Can you teach a Bible verse or Bible story to someone in your family? Do you have a little brother or sister you can help learn a Bible verse? Teach them today. You may grow up to be a Lincoln or a Timothy too! Pray for family members who haven't heard about Jesus.

Your Turn

1. Do the people in your family know God?
2. Ask your mother and father how they learned about God when they were little.

_____

_____

_____

_____

Prayer

Dear God, I am glad I know You. Help me tell people who don't know who You are. Amen.

Doing What Is Right

Do what is right and good in the LORD's sight.
– Deuteronomy 6:18

Bible Teaching Plan

Pretend you are Lois or Eunice teaching Timothy about God. Hand motions can help you learn and teach Bible verses. Learn the words and hand motions for Psalm 28:7. Teach them to a brother, sister, cousin, or friend. You can even perform it for your mom and dad.

You can also make up hand motions for other Bible verses.

The Lord   **Strength**

Is My   **and My Shield**

Prayer

Jesus, I know that it is right to tell people about You. Please give me the words to say so they will understand that You died for them and want to be their Savior. Amen.

125

Doing What Is Right

Do what is right and good in the LORD's sight.
– Deuteronomy 6:18

Grocery Store Scramble

Look at the words in the jars. The words are from Psalm 122:1. Copy the message on the sign in front of the store to help you remember them.

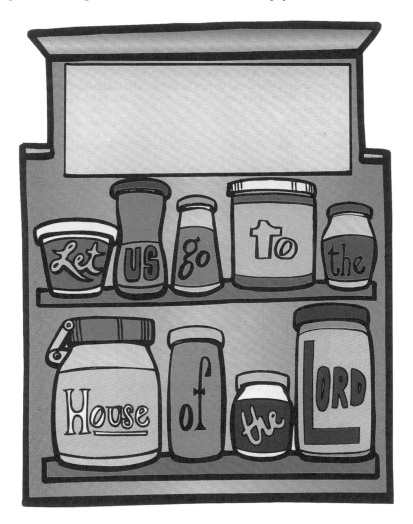

Prayer

God, I want to go to church so I can learn more about You and the Bible. Thank You for dying on the cross to save me. Amen.

126

Doing What Is Right

Do what is right and good in the LORD's sight.
– Deuteronomy 6:18

Your Playhouse

Do you go to Sunday school and church? Are there days when you would rather stay home? Everyone feels that way sometimes. In the house, write the things that might keep you from going to church to learn about Jesus. Ask God to help you go to church and grow strong in Him.

Prayer

Dear God, help me love going to Your house to learn more about You and to be with people who love You. Amen.

Growing in Jesus

Grow in the grace and knowledge of our
LORD and Savior Jesus Christ.
– 2 Peter 3:18

Growing in Faith

Dee wanted to follow her older sister wherever she went. "May I go skating with you?" Dee asked her older sister.

"No," her sister said. "You are too little."

"May I go to the movies with you?" asked Dee.

"No, you are too little."

"May I go to the basketball game with you?"

"No, you are too little."

Will I ever grow up and do something fun? Dee wondered.

Dee is growing all the time—and so are you. You may be too young to do some things now, but you will grow up and do them. One thing you can do right now is learn more about Jesus. This is called "growing in Jesus" or "growing in the grace and knowledge of Jesus."

Believing in Jesus means you have faith in Him. Faith is believing God loves you. Faith is believing God forgives your sins when you are sorry. Faith is knowing you are God's child. Your faith in Jesus and God will grow when you study the Bible and go to church and Sunday school.

Your Turn

1. What are some ways you can keep learning about Jesus?
2. What will you read in your Bible each day this week?

_____

_____

_____

Prayer

Jesus, I want to keep growing as Your follower. Please increase my faith and my knowledge of You. Amen.

Growing in Jesus

Grow in the grace and knowledge of our
LORD and Savior Jesus Christ.
– 2 Peter 3:18

Growth Chart

Dee wanted to do everything her older sister was doing, but she was too young. Are there things you want to do, but you are too little? Jesus knows you cannot do everything right now. First He wants you to grow and learn. Then you can do things like go to church camp.

Look at the bottom of the growth chart. On the two bottom lines, write things you can do now. Now look at the top of the growth chart. On lines four and three, write two things you will be able to do when you get older.

4. _____

_____

_____

_____

3. _____

_____

_____

2. _____

_____

_____

1. _____

_____

_____

Prayer

Dear God, I know there are things I can do for You today. Thank You. I also know that as I learn more about You, I'll be able to do even more for You. Hooray! Amen.

Growing in Jesus

Grow in the grace and knowledge of our
LORD and Savior Jesus Christ.
– 2 Peter 3:18

Knock Knock

Make up a knock-knock joke that might cheer up someone and tell them about God. Here is an example:

Knock, knock.   Who's there?   Godso.

Godso who?   God so loves the world and you!

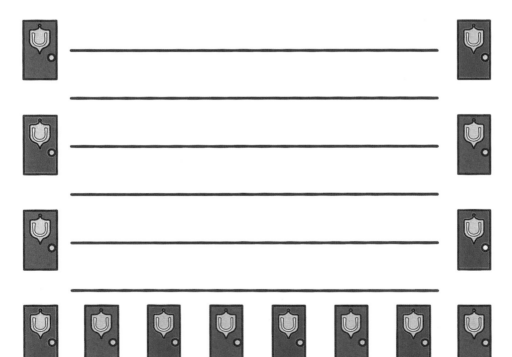

_____

_____

_____

_____

_____

Prayer

Dear God, You put gladness in my heart. I want to share Your joy with people I care about. Amen.

Growing in Jesus

Grow in the grace and knowledge of our
LORD and Savior Jesus Christ.
– 2 Peter 3:18

Being Strong

My daddy is the strongest man in the world, Abby thought. She was watching him lift her little sister Lora way up in the air. Many times Abby also saw him lifting heavy things when he did work around the house.

One day Abby asked, "How strong are you, Daddy? Can you come to my room and move my desk? I can't do it because it is big."

"Sure, I will help you! We will do it together," he said.

"After we move the desk, will you help with my math paper?" asked Abby.

"Yes, honey, we can also do math together."

Abby's dad told her to put her hands on the desk. He stood behind her, placing his hands next to hers. Together they moved the desk.

We all need help sometimes. God will always help you. He may not move your desk for you, but He might send someone who helps you. He will always help you learn and grow to be the person He wants you to be.

Your Turn

1. Why couldn't Abby move the desk by herself?
2. Who has God sent to help you do things you can't do by yourself?

_____

_____

_____

_____

Prayer

Dear Jesus, I know You are my Friend and my Helper. With Your help I can do anything You want me to. Amen.

Growing in Jesus

Grow in the grace and knowledge of our
LORD and Savior Jesus Christ.
– 2 Peter 3:18

God's Hands

Trace your hand on the X below God's hand. On your hand, write down something you need help to do. Now ask God to help you.

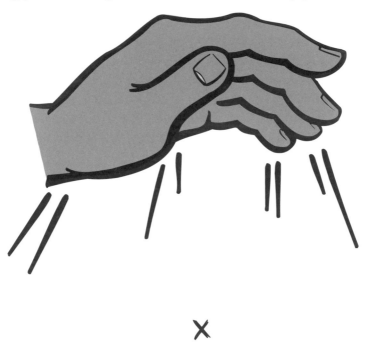

X

Prayer

Dear LORD, thank You for always being here for me. You give me strength. Amen.

Growing in Jesus

Grow in the grace and knowledge of our
LORD and Savior Jesus Christ.
– 2 Peter 3:18

Wonderful Me Clips

God made you special for a reason. Do you love who you are? God sure does! On the left side, draw a picture of you when you were a baby. On the right side, draw a picture of you today. See how much you've grown?

Prayer

Thank You, God, for creating me. I am wonderfully made so I can serve You. Help me be strong. Amen.

Growing in Jesus

Grow in the grace and knowledge of our
LORD and Savior Jesus Christ.
– 2 Peter 3:18

Pleasing God

You may not be a princess with a crown. But you are important to Jesus! Jesus said, "Anyone who wants to be first (important) must be . . . the servant of all" (Mark 9:35). So if we want to be important or great for God, James tells us to serve God and receive "the crown of life." By serving God and helping people know His great love and mercy, you make God's heart happy! Write on the crown some ways you can be a servant for God.

Prayer

LORD Jesus, I am glad I know You. Help me do everything for You and not for me. Amen.

You Are God's Friend

Let us draw near to God with a sincere heart.
– Hebrews 10:22

Let God Pass By...

Kayla liked Angie from the day she met her. She wanted to be friends. Kayla told her mom, "I met a girl named Angie. I want to be her friend, but I'm just not sure how to do that. I feel like she doesn't even see me."

"Well, honey, just be friendly and be yourself. Maybe you can invite her over this Saturday," Mom said.

"That's a good idea, Mom!" Kayla said.

Moses was God's friend. "The LORD would speak to Moses face to face, as one speaks to a friend" (Exodus 33:11). Moses said to God, "Show me your glory." God told him, "I will cause all my goodness to pass in front of you." Then He said, "You cannot see my face, for no one may see me and live...When my glory passes by, I will put you in a cleft in the rock and cover you with my hand until I have passed by. Then I will remove my hand and you will see my back" (verse 22).

Do you know God wants you to know Him? He is waiting for you to invite Him into your heart.

Your Turn

1. God knew Moses well. How do you know God knows you, too?
2. What things help you to think about and pray to God?

_____

_____

_____

_____

Prayer

Dear God, I am asking You to come into my life. I want to know You and be Your friend. Amen.

You Are God's Friend

Let us draw near to God with a sincere heart.
– Hebrews 10:22

God's Cave Girl

God told Moses to stand in the cleft of a rock as He passed by. A cleft is kind of like a cave. List in the cave some things that will help you draw closer to God. Then see if you can fill in the missing words by memory. (Hint: It's this week's verse.)

Let us draw _____

to God with a sincere _____.

Prayer

Dear God, I want to be friends with You all the days of my life. Amen.

136

You Are God's Friend

Let us draw near to God with a sincere heart.

– Hebrews 10:22

Soapy Puzzle

Jamie was washing dishes when she lost her ring. She "exclaimed, "Oh no! What will I do?" Her mom said, "Let's ask God to help you find it." They asked and then Jamie searched the water and found her ring!

Circle the ring in the sink. At the bottom of the page, write down other things you can trust God for in your life.

I will trust God and Jesus to _____

_____

_____.

Prayer

God, I trust You in everything. There is nothing too big or too small for You. Amen.

You Are God's Friend

Let us draw near to God with a sincere heart.
– Hebrews 10:22

God's Princess Bride

Kaley watched as her big sister, Carrie, entered the room in her wedding dress. "Wow!" exclaimed Kaley. "You look like a princess!"

Carrie smiled at Kaley. "I feel like a princess today, little sis! I can't wait to marry Mike, my bridegroom and prince."

"I want to be a princess bride someday too," said Kaley.

"You'll be a bride even if you don't get married," said their mom.

"What do you mean?" Kaley asked.

"When you know Jesus, you become like His bride," her mom explained. "A husband and wife have a powerful love. God has that kind of powerful love for you. God's design for you is to grow closer in loving friendship with Him. Sin breaks that friendship, but God never gives up on His purposes for you. He sent Jesus to die for your sins. Once your sins are forgiven, you can know your bridegroom Jesus."

"I get it!" said Kaley. "God chose weddings to show us that He wants to come close to us."

"That's right," Mom said as she smiled and hugged her daughters.

Your Turn

1. Why do you think Kaley wanted to be a bride?
2. How does being God's bride make you feel about yourself?

_____

_____

_____

_____

Prayer

Dear God, You make me feel special and loved. Your powerful love makes me feel like a princess. Amen.

You Are God's Friend

Let us draw near to God with a sincere heart.
– Hebrews 10:22

Heart Puzzle

Solve the puzzle in the heart. Now copy the heart and hang it up in your room where you will see it every day.

1 2 3 4 5 6 7 8 9 10 11 12 13 14 15 16 17 18 19 20 21 22 23 24 25 26
A B C D E F G H I J K L M N O P Q R S T U V W X Y Z

$$\overline{7}\ \overline{15}\ \overline{4}\quad \overline{12}\ \overline{15}\ \overline{22}\ \overline{5}\ \overline{19}\quad \overline{13}\ \overline{5}!$$

Prayer

Dear God, I know Your love is powerful. Thank You for loving me. Amen.

You Are God's Friend

Let us draw near to God with a sincere heart.

– Hebrews 10:22

The Goad Secret

A goad is a stick with a point on the end. In Bible times, farmers used goads to help guide their oxen when plowing the fields. The Bible is God's powerful goad to poke your heart and mind so you will follow Him. Decode the goads below. The secret tells you what to do when God prods you to move.

A	B	C	D	E	F	G	H	I	J
1	2	3	4	5	6	7	8	9	10

K	L	M	N	O	P	Q	R	S	T
11	12	13	14	15	16	17	18	19	20

U	V	W	X	Y	Z
21	22	23	24	25	26

15 2 5 25   7 15 4 19

___ ___ ___ ___   ___ ___ ___ ___ ,

7 15 1 4

___ ___ ___ ___

Prayer

Dear God, help me know and feel Your guidance. Amen.

You Are God's Friend

Let us draw near to God with a sincere heart.
– Hebrews 10:22

Powerful Messages

On the chalkboard, write your own powerful message telling God how much you love Him.

Prayer

God, I am so thankful for Your power and truth. Teach me Your Word so I can draw closer to You. Amen.

God Knows What's Best

*God is working in you, giving you the desire and
the power to do what pleases him.*
– Philippians 2:13 NLT

The Opposite News

Anna's mother arrived home from the hospital with Anna's new brother. Anna couldn't wait to hold him.

"He's so cute!" she said with joy when she saw him.

The whole family was happy until the phone rang. Anna's dad hung up the phone with tears in his eyes.

"My mom has cancer," said Dad.

"What's cancer?" asked Anna.

"Cancer is a bad sickness," said Dad. He wiped his eyes. "Your grandma needs an operation."

"I am so sorry for Grandma's bad news," said Mom. "It is a good-news day for us but a bad-news day for Grandma."

"But this is our happy day!" said Anna. "Why can't God just make Grandma well?" she asked.

"I don't know, honey," Dad replied. "He might do that. But whether it is a good news day or a bad news day, God is in control. He makes good things out of what seem like bad things."

"That's true," agreed Mom. "God loves Grandma. He is at work in this problem. Let's pray and thank God right now for what He is going to do,"

Your Turn

1. Has something good and bad happened to you at the same time?
2. What can you do when good and bad things happen together?

_____

_____

Prayer

Dear God, I know You love me in good times and bad. Help me trust Your plan. I know You are at work for my best. Amen.

God Knows What's Best

*God is working in you, giving you the desire and
the power to do what pleases him.*
– Philippians 2:13 NLT

God Is at Work

Isn't it comforting to know God is always at work to help you? Find and circle these words in the puzzle: GOD, IS, AT, WORK.

C R K W I S A
S O M H N E Y
G O N I N Z D
U O P T P D O
W C D A T H S
R L Q K J O T
W O R K Z V L

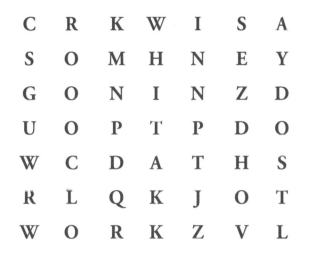
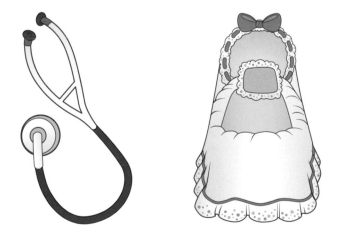

Prayer

Dear God, even when I don't understand, help me trust You that everything that happens in my life will be used for Your good purpose. Amen.

God Knows What's Best

*God is working in you, giving you the desire and
the power to do what pleases him.*
– Philippians 2:13 NLT

Creation Story Squares

Each story square shows one day of God's creation of the world. Look
at each picture and thank God for what He created. For example, on the
seventh square, you could say, "Thank You, God, for the trees. You are a
great God!"

Prayer

Dear God, thank You for creating such a wonderful world. Thank You
for creating me! Amen.

God Knows What's Best

*God is working in you, giving you the desire and
the power to do what pleases him.*
– Philippians 2:13 NLT

Power over the Sky

"God is powerful," said Rachel to Alison.

"Who is God?" asked Alison.

"He is my Father in heaven, and He is wonderful," replied Rachel.

In Bible times, a man named Joshua also knew the power of his Father in heaven. Joshua led the Israelites. He was also the commander of the army.

One time, Joshua and his soldiers had to fight five different armies in one battle! God told him, "Do not be afraid of them…for I have given you victory." Joshua's army marched all night to surprise the other armies. God helped the Israelite soldiers as He promised. He caused the other armies to panic and get confused. Then, when they ran away, big hailstones fell from the sky on top of them (Joshua 10). Joshua's army chased the enemy soldiers.

Then Joshua prayed to God, "Let the sun stand still." God made the sun stand still and the moon stop moving so Joshua's army could totally defeat their enemies.

Joshua told his soldiers, "Don't ever be afraid or discouraged…Be strong and courageous" (Joshua 10:25 NLT).

Your Turn

1. What is a time when you saw God's power?
2. What words can you use to describe God's power?

_____

_____

_____

Prayer

Dear God, I am glad You are powerful. I like the way You are both powerful and kind. Show me how to tell others of Your wonderful acts. Amen.

God Knows What's Best

God is working in you, giving you the desire and
the power to do what pleases him.
– Philippians 2:13 NLT

God's Power Dots

God created great things, including light. Connect the power dots. Write
the names of two friends in the pictures. Make plans to tell them about
your powerful God.

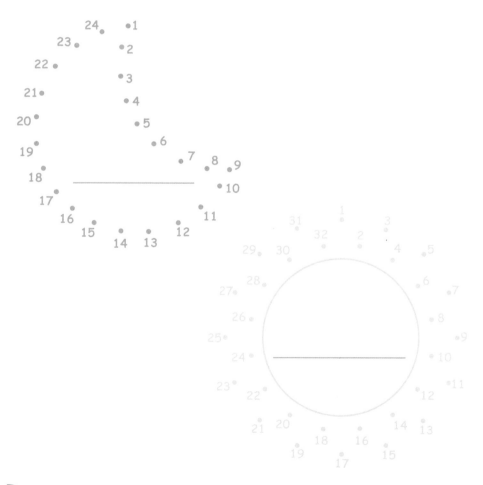

Prayer

Dear God, I praise Your name. I want to tell everyone about You. Amen.

God Knows What's Best

*God is working in you, giving you the desire and
the power to do what pleases him.*
– Philippians 2:13 NLT

Powerful Postcards

Sharing God's love with your friends is fun. Here is one way: Buy post- cards. Write fun notes to your friends about God on them. Ask your parents to mail them, or give them out. Use this practice postcard. Tell a friend how powerful God is and how much He loves your friend.

Prayer

Dear LORD, thank You for always looking out for my friends and me. I love You. Amen.

God Knows What's Best

*God is working in you, giving you the desire and
the power to do what pleases him.*
– Philippians 2:13 NLT

A Holy Mirror

Only God is perfect. But He tells us that because Jesus died and lives
again, He is at work in us. He makes us want to do what pleases Him—
and He gives us the power to do it! Write on the mirror what helps you
do what pleases Him. For example, you might write, "I pray and ask
God what to do."

Prayer

Dear God, I am glad You are holy and right. Help me do right and live
the way You want me to. Amen.

God's Amazing Power

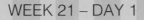

*Great and mighty God...great are your purposes
and mighty are your deeds.*

– Jeremiah 32:18-19

The Storm

Lora was visiting her Aunt Carol when a big storm blew in. Lightning struck close by, and the lights went out.

"I have an oil lamp," Aunt Carol said. She turned on a flashlight and found the lamp. She lit it before turning off the flashlight.

Lora snuggled close to her aunt.

Aunt Carol said, "The Bible tells many stories of God's power helping people."

"Tell me one," said Lora.

"The apostle Paul traveled to many places telling people about Jesus. Once, he was even arrested. The soldiers put him on a ship to Rome to be judged by the Roman ruler. A strong wind came, and the ship tossed, and turned, and bounced. The men threw cargo and equipment overboard so they wouldn't sink.

"For many days, the men couldn't see the sun or the stars. They were afraid. Then Paul told them an angel had appeared to him in the night and said they would all be safe. And they were!"

Lora was amazed. God was powerful, and she was no longer scared.

Your Turn

1. Where do you see God's power?
2. What can you do when you are scared?

_____

_____

_____

_____

Prayer

Dear God, Your power is wonderful. Remind me that You are with me when I am afraid. Amen.

God's Amazing Power

*Great and mighty God...great are your purposes
and mighty are your deeds.*

– Jeremiah 32:18-19

Weather Wheel

What kind of weather did Paul face in the story? What is your favorite
type of weather? In the weather wheel, draw a sun in one section, rain in
another, clouds in another, and a tree bending in the wind in the last one.
God created the weather!

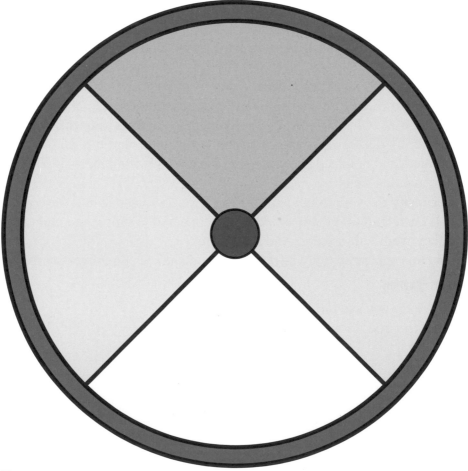

Prayer

Dear God, You are all-powerful, and I put my trust in You always.
Amen.

150

God's Amazing Power

Great and mighty God...great are your purposes
and mighty are your deeds.

– Jeremiah 32:18-19

Spilled Love

God has so much love for us that it fills us up, and then spills out all over!
He wants us to share His powerful love. Write ways God shows His love
for you on the heart shapes.

Prayer

Dear God, fill me with Your love and help me share it. Amen.

God's Amazing Power

*Great and mighty God...great are your purposes
and mighty are your deeds.*

– Jeremiah 32:18-19

Hands Up

"Raise your hand if you have a question," Mrs. Colby said.

One day, Kelly raised her hand, but Mrs. Colby didn't see her. Kelly's hand was in the air for a long, long time. *My arm feels like it will fall off!* she thought. Finally her name was called. *Whew!* she thought.

Once, God's friend Moses had to keep his hands up—but not to get a question answered. An enemy army was coming. Moses called for Joshua, the army commander. "Choose some men for battle," Moses said. "I'll stand on the hill and watch."

Joshua did as Moses said, and Moses went up the hill with Aaron and Hur. They watched the battle. When Moses held up his hands, God's people would win. When Moses lowered his hands, the enemy would win.

Moses' arms got so tired that Aaron and Hur helped hold Moses' hands high from morning until night. Joshua and God's army won the battle!

God used Aaron and Hur to help Moses. God will help you do the right thing when you are tired.

Your Turn

1. Name some of your friends God might use to help you.
2. Think of a time when you were weak. How did God help?

_____

_____

_____

Prayer

God, You are my helper. Help me trust in You when I am weak. Amen.

God's Amazing Power

*Great and mighty God...great are your purposes
and mighty are your deeds.*

– Jeremiah 32:18-19

Arm Writing

Who has God used to help you do something special? Think of two people
and write their names on the girl's arm below. Pray and thank God for
your own "Aaron" and "Hur."

Prayer

God, You are always ready with Your power to help me. I know I don't
have to worry when I am weak because You are beside me. Amen.

153

God's Amazing Power

*Great and mighty God...great are your purposes
and mighty are your deeds.*

– Jeremiah 32:18-19

Winding Problems

Write a problem on the winding river. Pray for God's help. Remember, God always knows what's best. He may not answer in exactly the way you want, but He has a plan for your life and will do what is right and best for you. When God answers, write that on the river too.

Prayer

Dear God, I'm glad You can do anything and that You are powerful. Thank You for answering my prayers. Amen.

154

God's Amazing Power

*Great and mighty God...great are your purposes
and mighty are your deeds.*

– Jeremiah 32:18-19

Your Prayer List

What do you need from God besides food and water? Make your own list
of what you need and pray God will meet them.

Prayer List

1.

2.

3.

4.

5.

6.

7.

8.

Prayer

Dear God, thank You for Your love and care. Amen.

Serving God and People

God is near us whenever we pray to him.
– Deuteronomy 4:7

Prayers Upstairs

Jennifer and Mom were cleaning the spare room. Mom said, "I feel God wants us to turn this into a bedroom for your grandma."

"Yes!" said Jennifer. "With a table here and a bed over there." She paused. "I sound like the woman I learned about in Sunday school."

"Tell me about her," Mom said.

Jennifer said, "The story is in 2 Kings 4. A woman of Shunem knew God. One day God's prophet Elisha went to the woman's town. She asked him to come for dinner. Soon Elisha stopped to eat there whenever he came by.

"The woman got an idea and told her husband, 'Let's make a small room on the roof. We'll put a bed and a table, a chair and a lamp in it for Elisha.' "

"When Elisha saw the room, he was very happy. He wanted to do something for the man and woman. The woman didn't have a child, so Elisha told her she would have a son by that time next year—and she did!"

"God can do anything!" Mom said.

Your Turn

1. List three things you can do to help people.
2. Make a plan for how you will do those three things—and then, do them.

_____

_____

Prayer

God, I want to be a girl who prays. Let me hear Your voice and follow You. Amen.

Serving God and People

God is near us whenever we pray to him.
– Deuteronomy 4:7

Prayer Room

Do you have a special place where you pray? If not, find one. It doesn't have to be a room or closet, just someplace quiet and peaceful. Make sure your parents know where it is. Now, write a prayer you can pray in your special prayer place.

_____

_____

_____

_____

Prayer

Dear God, help me develop the habit of prayer. I know You hear me and answer. Thank You! Amen.

Serving God and People

God is near us whenever we pray to him.
– Deuteronomy 4:7

Your Big Prayer Page

Write some big prayer requests on the prayer page. Remember, God answers big prayers and small prayers.

My Prayer Requests

Prayer

Thank You, God, for hearing my big and small prayers. I know You will answer! Amen.

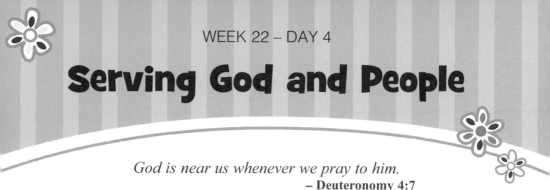

Serving God and People

God is near us whenever we pray to him.
– Deuteronomy 4:7

A Path of Prayer

Brett challenged his little sister, Amelia, to a bike ride. They would ride down Deer Trail, the prettiest path in Fall City. Oak and maple trees spread like giant umbrellas over the stones along the path. Curves made the three-mile course fun.

Brett wondered if Amelia could ride to the end without stopping. She was young, but she was energetic. She loved riding bikes and climbing trees.

Amelia surprised Brett by riding the Deer Trail as far as "Old Mulberry." That old tree was the start of the "Mulberry Mile," the last mile on the trail. Amelia couldn't go any further. She had to stop and rest.

"Don't stop! Let's keep going!" Brett called. "Don't give up."

A woman named Anna traveled a trail of prayer. Unlike Amelia on Deer Trail, Anna never rested. Her husband had died, and she never married again. Instead, she set out on a path of worshiping God through prayer and fasting (Luke 2:36-38). God blessed her devotion by allowing her to meet Joseph and Mary and their baby. Anna was one of the first people to tell others that Jesus was God's Son.

Your Turn

1. What things are hard for you to do?
2. This week, what would help you to pray a little longer than last week? Try it!

_____

_____

Prayer

God, I am glad You love me and let me talk to You. Please help me remember to pray every day. Amen.

Serving God and People

God is near us whenever we pray to him.
– Deuteronomy 4:7

Deer Trail Prayers

Follow the prayers up and down the deer trail. Don't stop praying until you get to the end. Remember to be like Anna and pray every day.

Prayer

Dear God, thank You that because You love me I can always be joyful. Help me remember to pray and tell You about everything going on in my life. Amen.

Serving God and People

God is near us whenever we pray to him.
– Deuteronomy 4:7

The Heart Bank

Do you have a piggy bank or some kind of container where you save up your allowance? You can think about memories the same way. You can store them in your heart. Think of a special time you had with Jesus. Draw a picture of it in the heart bank.

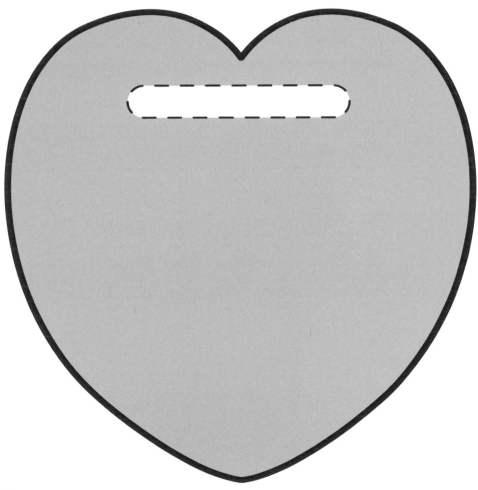

Prayer

Dear God, thank You for special times with You. I want to remember them always. Amen.

Serving God and People

God is near us whenever we pray to him.
– Deuteronomy 4:7

Hands to Heaven

Sometimes people choose to give up something as part of their prayers. This is called fasting. Jesus talked about fasting (Matthew 6:16-18). Think of something you can give up for three days to and take that extra time to pray. You might choose to skip a favorite TV program or go without soda. Write one thing you will give up on each of the three prayer hands below. When you fast, do it in secret. Make fasting a commitment between you and God and your parents.

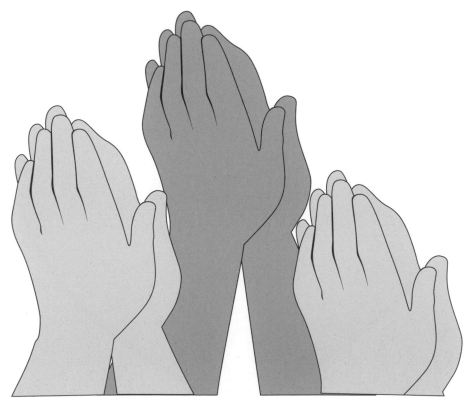

Prayer

Dear God, thank You for answering my prayers. Thank You for being with me all the time. Amen.

Put on God's Armor

Be strong in the LORD and in his mighty power.
Put on the full armor of God.

– Ephesians 6:10-11

Getting Dressed

"Hurry! It's time for breakfast and school," Mom said.

"What should I wear?" Gina asked.

"Something warm," said Mom. "It's cold outside."

"Okay!" Gina thought for a minute. "I'll wear my belt, put on a vest, and wear my boots."

"Don't forget your jacket and hat!" Mom called.

Gina looked in the mirror. "I almost forgot my Bible!"

When you get up, you put on clothes. God has something special for you to put on too—His armor.

This armor includes the "belt of truth," the "breastplate of righteousness," the "helmet of salvation," the "shield of faith," the "shoes of peace" and the "sword of the Spirit" (Ephesians 6:10-18). This armor is not something you can see. But it is strong! Truth is like a belt that protects us. Jesus' righteousness is protection for our hearts. The helmet of salvation is remembering Jesus died for you. The sword of God's Spirit is God's Word. He helps us use it to overcome wrong.

God wants you pray and ask Him to put this armor on you each day. Then you are protected and ready for anything He asks you to do!

Your Turn

1. What does God's armor do for you?
2. What can you do to put on God's armor every day?

_____

_____

_____

Prayer

LORD, keep me close and remind me to put on Your armor. Amen.

Put on God's Armor

Be strong in the LORD *and in his mighty power.*
Put on the full armor of God.

– Ephesians 6:10-11

Armor Match

Read Ephesians 6:10-18. Match each piece of God's armor to what it means.

belt of truth

breastplate of righteousness

helmet of salvation

shield of faith

sword of the Spirit

good news of peace

Prayer

LORD, help me understand and put on Your armor so I can stand strong in You. Amen.

Put on God's Armor

Be strong in the LORD and in his mighty power.
Put on the full armor of God.

– Ephesians 6:10-11

Buckle Up

Complete the belt buckle. Remember how important telling the truth is to God, to your parents, and to you.

BUCKLE UP WITH...

THE _____

OF _____

Prayer

God, remind me to keep the belt of truth buckled around my waist at all times. Help me always tell the truth. Amen.

Put on God's Armor

Be strong in the LORD and in his mighty power.
Put on the full armor of God.

– Ephesians 6:10-11

Doing Right

Summer went to work with her mother one day. Summer noticed colored pens in her mother's desk drawer. She held up a pen. "May I take this home?"

"No, honey. I'm not allowed to take those pens home," said Mom. "You can use the pens when you come to work with me."

Summer wanted the purple pen. She waited until her mother left the room, and then reached into the drawer and pulled out the purple pen. She slipped it into her book bag. Later, her book bag fell over and the pen rolled out. Her mom saw the pen, and Summer was in trouble.

Ephesians 6:14 says, "Stand firm...with the breastplate of righteousness in place." The breastplate of righteousness protects your heart. It helps you make right choices.

Let this song help you remember the breastplate of righteousness, or doing right. Sing it to the tune of "Row, Row, Row Your Boat."

The Breastplate Song
Do, do, do what's right, do what's right today.
Always ask God for His help so you go the right way.

Your Turn

1. How can the breastplate of righteousness help you pick friends?

_____

_____

_____

Prayer

Dear God, remind me to wear the breastplate of righteousness. Teach me to make the best choices. Amen.

Put on God's Armor

*Be strong in the L*ORD *and in his mighty power.*
Put on the full armor of God.

– Ephesians 6:10-11

Vest Friends

Wearing the vest or breastplate of righteousness is important in making right choices. Write your friends' names on the vest below. Pray and ask God to give you more friends who will encourage you to stay close to Him.

Stand firm...with the
breastplate of
righteousness in place.
Ephesians 6:14

Prayer

Dear God, I want to put on Your breastplate of righteousness and make the best choices. Amen.

Put on God's Armor

Be strong in the LORD and in his mighty power.
Put on the full armor of God.

– Ephesians 6:10-11

Wearing Your Breastplate

Draw a breastplate on the girl to help her do the right things. Write on the breastplate some things you did right this week.

Prayer

Dear God, I belong to You. I want to be right with You and stay right with You. Amen.

Put on God's Armor

Be strong in the LORD and in his mighty power.
Put on the full armor of God.

– Ephesians 6:10-11

Jesus and You

When we pray and ask God to put His armor on us, we want to spend more time with Jesus. Draw yourself at Jesus' feet. Think of ways to get close to Jesus.

Prayer

Dear Jesus, thank You for loving me. Help me choose to be close to You by reading my Bible and talking to You in prayer. Amen.

169

Keeping the Peace

Make every effort to live in peace with everyone.
– Hebrews 12:14

The Greatest Peacemaker

Colleen and her mother didn't get along. They argued over big things like manners. They argued over little things like clothes.

Mom would say, "Colleen, you need to wear a sweater."

Colleen would say, "It's not cold, Mom! I don't want to wear a sweater." Colleen did not have peace with her mom.

Colleen's mom told Colleen, "You know I love you very much. Let's talk about how we can get along better. We need to live in peace with each other." Colleen's mom was a peacemaker.

The greatest Peacemaker is Jesus. He died so that people could have peace with God.

People who know Jesus can wear the shoes of peace. Wherever we walk, we can have peace inside us. Then we can help others be at peace. That is one way we wear God's armor to overcome what's wrong!

Your Turn

1. How does knowing Jesus help you make peace with others?
2. How can you be a peacemaker at school and home?

_____

_____

_____

_____

_____

Prayer

Dear God, help me encourage peace wherever I go. Amen.

Keeping the Peace

Make every effort to live in peace with everyone.

– Hebrews 12:14

Family Shoes

Write the names of your family members on the shoes. Pray for your family members and ask God to give them His shoes of peace.

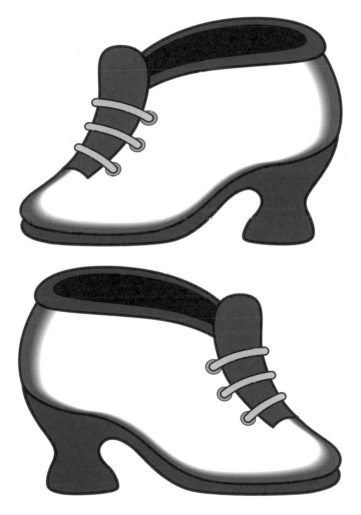

Prayer

Please help me, God, to be a peacemaker. I want to get along with people and tell them about the happiness they can have when they know You. Amen.

Keeping the Peace

Make every effort to live in peace with everyone.

– Hebrews 12:14

Your Boots

Draw boots on the girl. Write on the lines the people you want to make peace with and keep peace with.

_____

_____

_____

_____

Prayer

Dear God, teach me to wear Your boots of peace. Help me be Your peacemaker. Amen.

Keeping the Peace

Make every effort to live in peace with everyone.
– Hebrews 12:14

Shoes and Shield

Charlotte and her older brother were watching TV. A girl in the show wanted to pick a fight with another girl. It wasn't over anything very important, but she still wanted to fight.

"They shouldn't fight," said Charlotte. "Especially over something so silly."

Tommy muted the television. "Fighting isn't a good way to show your faith in Jesus, either. They need to wear shoes of peace and hold up their shields of faith."

"What is a shield of faith?" asked Charlotte.

Charlotte's brother rolled his eyes. "I told you before. It's part of God's armor for us. God's shield keeps belief in Jesus close to your heart and repels sin."

"I want to wear the shield of faith," said Charlotte.

"Good!" said her brother. He clicked the control to turn on the TV sound. "Now, let's watch the rest of the show and see if the girl changes her mind about fighting."

Your Turn

1. What is a good way to show someone you love Jesus?
2. How will shoes of peace and the shield faith help you?

_____

_____

_____

Prayer

Dear LORD, I believe You are my God and Savior. Forgive me for not always showing that I believe in You. Help me show my faith in You. I will put on the shield of faith. Amen.

Keeping the Peace

Make every effort to live in peace with everyone.
– Hebrews 12:14

Your Shield

Color your shield of faith. Write on the shield the things or people you have faith in. Don't forget Jesus!

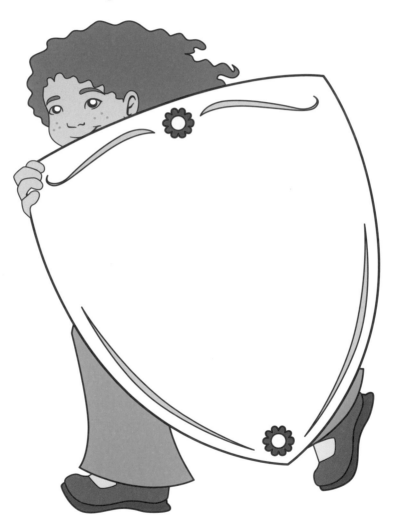

Prayer

Dear God, I want Your shield of faith. I know I need to read Your Word to make it strong. Please help me make a habit of Bible study. Amen.

174

Keeping the Peace

Make every effort to live in peace with everyone.
– Hebrews 12:14

Hat Game

WHAT YOU NEED: • a penny • a dried bean • this page
• two dice (or you can share one die)

Use a bean and a penny as markers to play the game with a friend. Roll a die, move that many spaces, and then share how you used the armor this week or how you will use it next week.

Prayer

Dear God, teach me to protect my mind and thoughts. Help me think good thoughts about the people around me. Amen.

Keeping the Peace

Make every effort to live in peace with everyone.
– Hebrews 12:14

A Good-Thinking Cap

On the thinking helmet, write or draw a picture of what Jesus would want you to think when you are wearing the helmet of salvation. Look up Philippians 4:8 for help.

Prayer

Dear LORD, I am sorry for not always wearing the helmet of salvation. Teach me to put it on and think like Jesus every day. Amen.

You Are Safe with Jesus

It's better to take refuge in the LORD than to trust in humans.

– Psalm 118:8

Titanic Trust

The *Titanic* was a huge passenger ship people thought would never sink. On its first journey from England to the United States, the people on board were eating, dancing, laughing, and sleeping. Then the *Titanic* struck an iceberg. This supposedly unsinkable ship sank within three hours. Because there weren't enough lifeboats, many people died in the cold ocean.

The *Challenger* and *Columbia* were space shuttles that blew up within seconds after lifting off. The *Columbia* exploded within seconds of returning to earth's atmosphere. Every crew member on both shuttles was killed.

In these situations, the most advanced technology at the time turned into huge failures.

Jesus is different. He is totally trustworthy. His friends learned to put their trust in Him rather than ordinary humans. Crossing the lake in a boat, a large storm surprised the disciples. The storm blew around them and waves crashed against the boat. Jesus slept while His friends worried. They were so afraid they woke Him. Jesus stood up and spoke to the storm. "Be still," He said. The winds died down and everything was calm.

Your Turn

1. Do you trust Jesus?
2. How can Jesus help you feel safe?

_____

_____

Prayer

Dear Jesus, help me know You and Your ways. Teach me to trust totally in You. Amen.

You Are Safe with Jesus

It's better to take refuge in the LORD than to trust in humans.

– Psalm 118:8

A Safe Ride

Draw a picture of your friends and you in the boat with Jesus.

Prayer

Dear Jesus, I am so glad You are my Savior. I trust You with my life, and I know You always want the best for me. Amen.

You Are Safe with Jesus

It's better to take refuge in the LORD than to trust in humans.
– Psalm 118:8

Breakfast with Jesus

Jesus surprised some of His friends by building a campfire and meeting them after they went fishing. Write on the campfire some places you go each week. This week as you do those things, think about Jesus being near even when you're not looking for Him. Draw yourself having breakfast with Jesus.

Prayer

Thank You, Jesus, for being near me always. You make me feel safe and happy. Remind me to think of You when I'm at school and at home. Amen.

You Are Safe with Jesus

It's better to take refuge in the LORD than to trust in humans.

– Psalm 118:8

"Knowsy" Jesus!

Casey was angry because her father corrected her table manners. *I'm mad. I wish I had a different family,* she thought.

Casey's family didn't know what she was thinking, but Jesus knew. He knows everything people think, and He sees everything people do. He knows the good things and the bad things. Jesus is "knowsy" in a good way because of His love.

Noelle's mom said, "Noelle, time for bed."

"I don't want to go to bed," Noelle said. "May I have a snack first?"

"You had a chance to eat at dinner. Get your pajamas on, brush your teeth, and get into bed," said Mom.

"Okay, Mom!" Noelle called. But she didn't go into the bathroom. Instead, she tiptoed into the kitchen and took some cookies from the cookie jar.

Even though Noelle's mom didn't catch her sneaking cookies, "knowsy" Jesus saw what she was doing.

Jesus knows everything, good and bad. What is wonderful is that He's ready to forgive you when you ask because He loves you.

Your Turn

1. What is good about Jesus being "knowsy"?
2. What is something you might do or not do when you remember Jesus knows and loves you?

_____

_____

_____

Prayer

LORD, please help me think and act the way You want me to. Amen.

You Are Safe with Jesus

It's better to take refuge in the Lord than to trust in humans.

– Psalm 118:8

Knowsy Puzzle

Solve the puzzle using the code to discover an important truth.

1	2	3	4	5	6	7	8	9	10	11	12	13	14	15	16	17	18	19	20	21	22	23	24	25	26
A	B	C	D	E	F	G	H	I	J	K	L	M	N	O	P	Q	R	S	T	U	V	W	X	Y	Z

___ ___ ___ ___ ,   ___ ___ ___   ___ ___ ___ ___   ___ ___ ___   ___ ___ ___ ___ ___ ___
12 15 18 4   25 15 21   11 14 15 23   1 12 12   20 8 9 14 7 19

– John 21:17

Prayer

Dear Lord, I am glad You know everything because it helps me want to do the right things. Thank You that when I do something wrong, You are quick to forgive me when I ask. Amen.

You Are Safe with Jesus

It's better to take refuge in the LORD than to trust in humans.
– Psalm 118:8

Mix and Serve

When you feel safe, you are more willing to help someone. On the mixing bowl, write the names of the people you will serve this week. After you serve each person, put a line through his or her name.

1. _____
2. _____
3. _____
4. _____

Prayer

Dear Jesus, thank You for making me feel safe so I can help You by helping others. Amen.

You Are Safe with Jesus

*It's better to take refuge in the L*ORD *than to trust in humans.*
– Psalm 118:8

The Fence

When you show kindness and love to someone, it has a special name. Use the code below the fence to solve the puzzle. You'll discover what Jesus wants to give you.

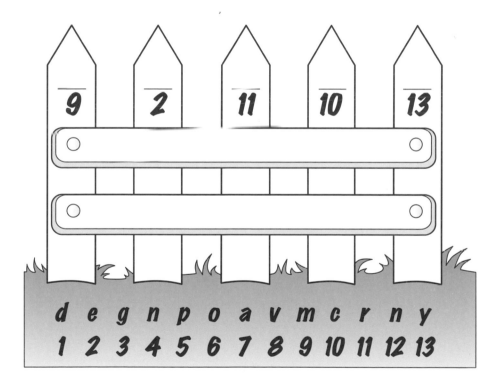

Prayer

Dear Jesus, thank You for Your love and mercy. Help me to show Your mercy to others. Amen.

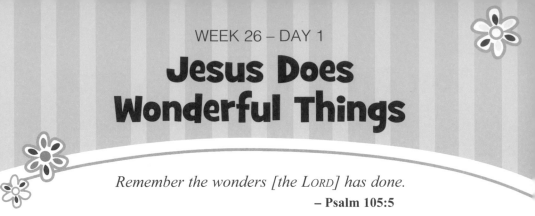

Jesus Does Wonderful Things

Remember the wonders [the LORD] has done.
– Psalm 105:5

A Report on Jesus

"My dad is wonderful because he can hit the ball over the fence," Kate wrote in her school report about the most wonderful person she knew. In her mind, Kate's dad was by far the strongest and best. He could fix her bike, paint her toy shelf, and put the wheel back on her scooter. He could even do all those things in one day.

Jesus is even more worthy of writing about! He is mighty because He can do anything and everything. The Bible tells of Jesus' great works. He healed the sick and fed the poor. He made the dead come to life again. He healed so the blind could see and the crippled could walk. Jesus walked on water and calmed a storm.

Making reports about your memories of family and friends is important and good. But the Bible reminds us to also report to others about how wonderful Jesus is and what He did—died on the cross for everyone's sins. Jesus rose from the dead to offer everyone forgiveness and eternal life. Remember His great works. Let Him work in your heart today and every day.

Your Turn

1. Why did Kate think her dad was terrific?
2. What are some wonderful things Jesus has done for you?
3. What might Jesus do for you today?

_____

_____

_____

Prayer

Dear Jesus, help me remember who You are and what You have done. You are wonderful. Amen.

Jesus Does Wonderful Things

Remember the wonders [the LORD] has done.

– Psalm 105:5

A Picture Report

On the left side of the report, draw a picture of someone in your family doing something you want to remember. On the right side, draw a picture of what you want to remember about Jesus.

Prayer

Dear Jesus, help me never forget the wonderful things You have done in my life. I am excited about what You will do today and tomorrow. Amen.

Jesus Does Wonderful Things

Remember the wonders [the LORD] has done.

– Psalm 105:5

Behind a Powerful Tug

Have you ever seen a tugboat at work? The tugboat and crew guide huge ships safely into harbors and up and down rivers. You can think of Jesus as a tugboat because if you ask, He will guide your family and you through life.

In each of the ship's portholes or windows, draw the face of one of your family members. If you need to, draw another boat so everyone in your family can be included.

Prayer

Dear God, thank You for Your love. Please guide my family so we will be safe in You. Amen.

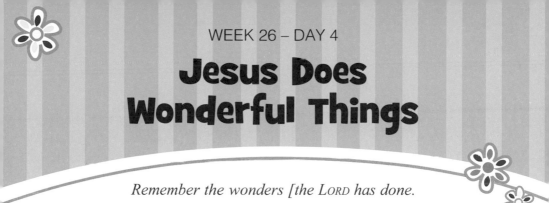

Jesus Does Wonderful Things

Remember the wonders [the LORD has done.
– Psalm 105:5

Being in God's House

"Christina, it's time for supper!" called Mom.

"Christina isn't here, Mom. She's at the church," said her brother Mike.

"She's just about lived at church this week," Mike said.

Mom smiled. "Being in God's house makes her feel close to Him."

"But you don't need to go to church to feel close to Jesus," said Mike.

"That's true," Mom said. "But Christina always says, 'It's just Jesus and me when I'm at church.' Jesus liked being at the Jewish temple when He was a boy."

Do you remember that story? Jesus' family went to Jerusalem for a special occasion. When it was over, they headed for home. Joseph and Mary thought Jesus was somewhere within their traveling group. When they realized Jesus was missing, they asked their friends where Jesus was. No one knew. Alarmed, they went back to Jerusalem. Finally, they found Him in the Jewish temple. He was sitting with the Bible teachers asking questions. Everyone was amazed at how much Jesus knew about God.

Your Turn

1. Why did Jesus like to go to the temple?
2. Why do you like going to church and Sunday school?

_____

_____

_____

Prayer

Dear God, I want to be with You in Your house so I can learn more about You. Amen.

Jesus Does Wonderful Things

Remember the wonders [the LORD] has done.

– Psalm 105:5

From Home to Church

Draw a line from the house to the church. Circle your favorite things to do at church or pick something new you would like to try.

Prayer

Dear God, I love going to church because I learn new things about You. You are amazing! Amen.

Jesus Does Wonderful Things

Remember the wonders [the LORD] has done.

– Psalm 105:5

Your Giving Calendar

Most churches support missionaries who tell people about Jesus. Churches also help people who might not have enough food or clothes. You can help people too! Write something you will do each day of the week to help someone in need. You can donate some of your toys, offer to make some cookies, and tell people you'll pray for them—and then do it.

Prayer

Dear God, help me find ways to give to people every day of the week. Amen.

Jesus Does Wonderful Things

Remember the wonders [the LORD] has done.
– Psalm 105:5

Exercising for Jesus

God created you, and He wants you to take care of your body. Exercise will make you strong and healthy. God also wants you to grow strong spiritually. You do that by exercising your mind by reading God's Word, praying, and going to church.

Look at the girls exercising their bodies. Think of an exercise for each one that will help her grow strong in God. Color the girls and then exercise with them.

Prayer

Dear Jesus, help me seek You with all my heart. I want to grow strong in body and spirit. Amen.

Experiencing Jesus Every Day

Taste and see that the LORD is good.
– Psalm 34:8

Taste and See Jesus

"Would you like some cake?" Mom asked Lily.

"Sure," said Lily. "But I want to taste a bit and see that it is good first."

"You just told me a Bible verse!" Mom said.

"What?" asked Lily.

"You said 'taste and see if the cake is good.'"

"The Bible says that?" Lily giggled.

"No." Mom laughed. "The Bible says, 'Taste and see that the LORD is good.'"

"I guess I did say a verse! What does it mean?" Lily asked.

"It means that Jesus our LORD is good and that the beautiful earth shows His goodness," Mom explained.

"Like green grass and blue sky?" asked Lily.

"Yes! There is a lot of the LORD's goodness out there," said Mom. "All of creation shows His goodness. So does everything you have. Remember the red bike you got for your birthday? That was the LORD's goodness. Your family, home, and friends are part of the LORD's goodness to you."

"Wow!" Lily said. "Jesus is better than a piece of cake."

Your Turn

1. What do you think it means to taste the goodness of Jesus?
2. Name three things that remind you that Jesus is with you.

_____

_____

_____

Prayer

Dear Jesus, Your goodness is all around me. Help me see You in everything that is good. Amen.

Experiencing Jesus Every Day

Taste and see that the LORD is good.

– Psalm 34:8

Jesus Goodies

Draw three of your favorite treats. Tell someone how these treats remind you of the goodness of Jesus in your life.

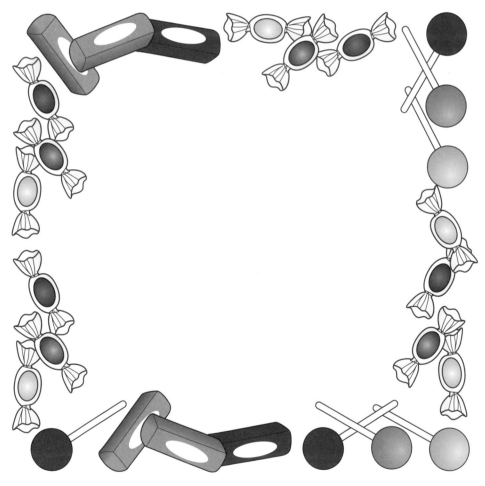

Prayer

Dear Jesus, I see Your goodness everywhere. I am so glad I know You! Amen.

Experiencing Jesus Every Day

Taste and see that the LORD is good.

– Psalm 34:8

The Word Keeper

Use the verse references to unscramble these verses. Write them below. Then read them aloud until you have memorized them!

_____

_____

_____

Prayer

Dear LORD Jesus, help me memorize Your Word so I will have it in my heart. Amen.

Experiencing Jesus Every Day

Taste and see that the LORD is good.

– Psalm 34:8

Follow the Leader

"Follow me!" said Miss Meyer, the Sunday-school teacher. Miss Meyer and the kids went in and out between chairs. Everyone marched out of the classroom, and down the hallway, and back again.

When they sat down for a snack, Miss Meyer said, "You did a great job following the leader. One thing you should know about this game is that we follow the best leader of all—Jesus Christ.

"The Bible says we should all be followers of Jesus. I led you to places in our building that made it hard to follow. In the hallway, it was kind of dark. In the classroom we went around chairs. That is the way it is when we follow Jesus. Sometimes life is hard, and we aren't always sure where we are going, but we can trust our Leader. "You see, Jesus is the Light of the world. Following Him leads you to good places and good choices. You follow Jesus by loving Him and doing the right things."

Your Turn

1. What can you do to follow Jesus?
2. What can you do when following Jesus seems difficult?

_____

_____

_____

_____

Prayer

Dear Jesus, help me follow You in all I do and say. I want to be Your follower, but I don't always know how. Please teach me to be Your disciple. Amen.

Experiencing Jesus Every Day

Taste and see that the LORD is good.

– Psalm 34:8

The Jesus Line

Follow Jesus! Draw yourself in the line behind Jesus. Draw your family and friends too.

Prayer

Dear Jesus, I want to follow You always because You are wonderful. Please help me stay close behind you. Amen.

Experiencing Jesus Every Day

*Taste and see that the L*ORD* is good.*

– Psalm 34:8

Your Savior and LORD

Jesus died for your sins and then rose from the dead so He could lead you to life everlasting with Him. He is your Savior and LORD. Think of some reasons why Jesus is *your* Leader and write them on the stone that was rolled away from His empty tomb.

Jesus is
my Leader
because...

Prayer

Dear Jesus, the more I learn about You, the more I love You. Thank You for being my Savior and LORD. Amen.

Experiencing Jesus Every Day

Taste and see that the LORD is good.

– Psalm 34:8

The Camp Road

Aren't you glad Jesus is your Leader? Draw a picture of your best friend and you walking on the road with Jesus.

Prayer

LORD, show me ways I can walk with You. Help me love others and be a good friend like You are to me. Amen.

Being Thankful for Jesus

[Jesus] loved me and gave himself for me.
– Galatians 2:20

A Dream

Lizzy wrote a beautiful poem:

At times dreams make me laugh; at times dreams make me cry.
It's fun to think about my dreams, as well as ask God why.

She was interested in dreams because hers were usually colorful and bright. But one night it wasn't. She ran into her parents' bedroom.

Mom said, "Lizzy, you had a nightmare."

"But it seemed real," Lizzy said. "It ended okay, but the middle was scary."

"That's how dreams are," said Dad. "It is like they are really happening. Tell us about your dream."

Lizzy sat down between her parents. "I was inside my playhouse having fun when it caught fire. I was trapped! I couldn't get out! Then a boy ran inside to get me out. I was fine, but he was hurt and disappeared. I never saw him again. I told everyone about the boy who saved me."

Mom smiled. "Lizzy, that's what Jesus did for you and me. He loved us so much that He let people hurt Him and kill Him. He gave up His life on Earth to save us from our sins. We will never forget what He did for us."

Your Turn

1. What are some ways you can tell Jesus "Thank You" for loving you so much?

_____

_____

_____

Prayer

Dear Jesus, I will never forget all You have done for me. Help me show You how thankful I am. Amen.

Being Thankful for Jesus

[Jesus] loved me and gave himself for me.
– Galatians 2:20

Creative Thanking

Design a creative "thank You" to Jesus for dying on the cross for you. Decorate the page for Him.

Prayer

Dear Jesus, I am so thankful You saved me. I want to tell You every day how grateful I am. Amen.

Being Thankful for Jesus

[Jesus] loved me and gave himself for me.
– Galatians 2:20

A Big Cross

Write your name and your friends' names on the cross. Pray for each person every day. Ask Jesus to save them or thank Him for those who already know Him.

Prayer

Dear Jesus, I love You for what You did on the cross. I thank You for rising from the dead so I can live with You forever. Amen.

Being Thankful for Jesus

[Jesus] loved me and gave himself for me.
– Galatians 2:20

The Clouds

"Look at the cloud in the sky!" said Laura.

"It looks like a sailboat," Sierra exclaimed.

Laura pointed to a cloud in a different direction. "Look at that one over there. It looks like a teddy bear."

Laura said, "The clouds remind me of what my Sunday-school teacher told us. She said Jesus left Earth in a cloud. He had led His friends to a place out of town. On the way, He told them the Holy Spirit would come and help them tell others about Him. Then Jesus went up in the air! Two angels appeared beside Jesus friends and told them that Jesus would come back the same way He left."

"Interesting," Sierra said.

"My Sunday-school teacher said Jesus wants us to share His love with others," Laura explained. "Jesus saved me, so I should share His love everywhere."

Sierra said, "Hey, Laura, may I come with you next Sunday?"

"That would be great!"

Your Turn

1. Why did Jesus send the Holy Spirit when He went to heaven?
2. How will you tell people about Jesus?

_____

_____

_____

Prayer

Thank You, Jesus, for sending the Holy Spirit to help me tell people about You. Amen.

Being Thankful for Jesus

[Jesus] loved me and gave himself for me.
– Galatians 2:20

Heart Clouds

Think of friends and acquaintances you know who don't know Jesus. Write their names in the heart cloud. Ask God to help you tell them about Jesus.

Prayer

Thank You, Jesus, for sending the Holy Spirit to help me. Give me opportunities to tell people about You. Amen.

Being Thankful for Jesus

[Jesus] loved me and gave himself for me.
– Galatians 2:20

Jesus' Strength

In ballet, the male dancers often gracefully lift the female dancers. As strong as the men are, they can't compare to Jesus. Jesus can take your sins away. On the ballerina's skirt, write some sins people want Jesus to take away. If you struggle with any of these sins, ask Jesus to take them away and fill you with His love and strength.

Prayer

Dear Jesus, forgive me for doing what I want to do rather than what You want me to do. Come into my life and fill me with You. Amen.

Being Thankful for Jesus

[Jesus] loved me and gave himself for me.
– Galatians 2:20

Sin Spots

Have you ever had chickenpox? It covers your body with red bumps that itch. Think of sin like chickenpox. If you don't ask Jesus to forgive you and take away your sins, sin will spread in your life.

Do you have "sin spots"? Jesus will take them away if you ask Him to forgive you. Draw the girl without the spots to show that Jesus can make sin go away if you ask Him.

Prayer

Jesus, thank You for helping me see my sin spots. Forgive me for my sins and take them away. Thank You! Amen.

Jesus Chose to Die for You

The Son of Man came to seek and to save the lost.
– Luke 19:10

Running to Jesus

In Bible times, the skin disease called leprosy was more common than it is today. Leprosy causes skin to turn white in patches and then die. Leprosy can be passed from one person to another, so in the ancient days lepers were forced to live outside the city walls. They often begged for food and money at the city gates.

Jesus and His disciples were traveling when a man with leprosy came running up. He knelt in front of Jesus and said, "LORD, if you are willing, you can make me clean" (Matthew 8:2).

Jesus touched the man and said, "I am willing…Be clean!"

Immediately the leprosy was gone! How happy the man was!

You probably don't have leprosy, but you have had times when you showed selfishness, envy, anger, and hatred. In a way that is like being sick—sick with sin. Just like the leper, you can run to Jesus for help. When you have a wrong attitude, or do something wrong, or think bad thoughts, run to Jesus and ask Him to take away your sin and make your heart clean. He is always willing.

Your Turn

1. What sin spots in your life do you want to talk to Jesus about?
2. What can Jesus do for your spots? Will you ask Him to?

_____

_____

_____

Prayer

Dear Jesus, I know I have sinned. Please forgive me and make my heart clean. Thank You. Amen.

Jesus Chose to Die for You

The Son of Man came to seek and to save the lost.

– Luke 19:10

A Jesus Run

The man with leprosy ran to met Jesus when he saw Him. You can run to Jesus whenever you want, night or day, morning or night. Start at the bottom of the maze and help the leper at the gate find his way to Jesus.

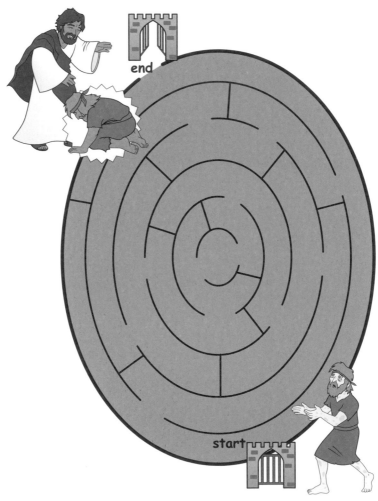

Prayer

Dear Jesus, I know everyone sins, including me. Please help me run to You quickly when I mess up. I want to ask You to forgive me. Amen.

Jesus Chose to Die for You

The Son of Man came to seek and to save the lost.

– Luke 19:10

Swim to Jesus

Have you ever been in a large swimming pool? If you don't swim very well, it can be scary. When you take swimming lessons, you trust your teacher to teach you to swim and keep you safe. You can trust Jesus to always be with you and watch over you.

The girl in the pool trusts Jesus and wants to swim to Him. Will you help her find her way?

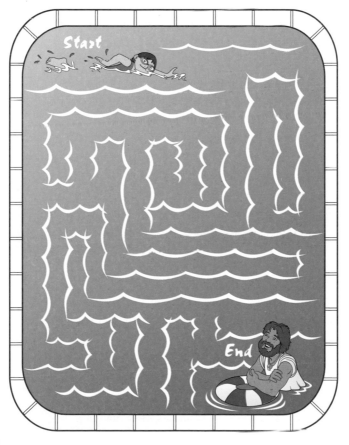

Prayer

Dear Jesus, I trust You. Help me love and trust You more and more every day. Amen.

Jesus Chose to Die for You

The Son of Man came to seek and to save the lost.
– Luke 19:10

The Blind Game

Rachel and Amanda loved to play "blind man." One girl tied a scarf over the other girl's eyes. Then the sighted girl led the blind girl around chairs and tables. They wanted to feel what it was like to be blind.

Dad said, "Girls, some people have sight but can't see."

"What do you mean, Dad?" asked Rachel.

Dad said, "We don't always see the things of God with our eyes. With Jesus, we learn to open the eyes of our hearts so we can understand more about God through His Word."

"I want my heart to be open to Jesus," Amanda and Rachel said.

In John 9, there's a story about a man who was born blind. "Why is this man blind?" Jesus' followers asked.

Jesus said, "So that the works of God might be displayed." Jesus spat on the ground. He made mud from the dirt and put it on the man's eyes. "Go wash in the pool of Siloam," said Jesus.

The man washed the mud off and he could see! When the man met Jesus again, he said, "LORD, I believe," and he worshiped Him.

The man's eyes were opened, and the eyes of his heart were also opened.

Your Turn

1. Thinking about Jesus and His love helps your heart to "see" Him.
   What are some things that help you to think about Jesus?

_____

_____

_____

Prayer

Dear Jesus, open my eyes and my heart so I can see and know You more each day. Amen.

Jesus Chose to Die for You

The Son of Man came to seek and to save the lost.

– Luke 19:10

My Heart's Eyes

Use a crayon to turn the blind heart into a seeing heart. Figure out the secret message at the bottom of the page using the code.

S	L	J	A	P	S	C	N	E	U	E	O	V
1	2	3	4	5	6	7	8	9	10	11	12	13

$\overline{2}\ \overline{12}\ \overline{13}\ \overline{9}$ $\overline{3}\ \overline{9}\ \overline{6}\ \overline{10}\ \overline{6}$.

Prayer

Dear Jesus, I know that before You saved me, my heart was blind to You and Your Word. Open my eyes and my heart so I can experience and share Your love. Amen.

Jesus Chose to Die for You

The Son of Man came to seek and to save the lost.
– Luke 19:10

Wing Drawings

Psalm 36:7 says, "How priceless is your unfailing love, O God! People take refuge in the shadow of your wings." Birds protect their young and guard them by hiding them under their wings. God's love is like a bird that spreads its wings to cover and protect its young. Draw yourself under the goose's wing to remind you that you are loved and protected by God.

Prayer

Thank You, Jesus, for loving me and protecting me. I love you! Amen.

Jesus Chose to Die for You

The Son of Man came to seek and to save the lost.
– Luke 19:10

Connect the Hearts

Connect the hearts for each letter to see a great message for you to remember.

Prayer

Thank You, Jesus, for dying for me and saving my soul. I will show my love for You by obeying and helping You. Amen.

211

You Are God's Child

*To those who believed in his name, [Jesus] gave
the right to become children of God.*

– John 1:12

A Child of God

Rosa's parents died when she was a baby, so she lived in a special home for children without parents. Rosa loved the adults who cared for her. She had everything she needed. But the one thing she wanted most was a real family. She felt empty inside her heart.

One day a man and woman visited the home where Rosa lived. The couple liked Rosa. Each time they came, they mostly talked to her. They visited Rosa many times and grew to love her very much.

"Soon we will come back for you and take you as our own child," they said.

The couple wants to adopt me! Rosa felt joy and hope rush into her heart.

When the special day finally came, Rosa left the home to begin a new life with her adoptive parents. She was so happy!

When you come to know Jesus as LORD and Savior, you are like Rosa because you are brought into God's big family. Just as the couple adopted Rosa, God chose to adopt you! But God doesn't take you away from your parents. He just adds you to His family.

Your Turn

1. Why are people happy when they come to know Jesus?
2. Have you been adopted by God?

_____

_____

_____

Prayer

Jesus, thank You for coming to die for me so I can be adopted into Your family. Amen.

You Are God's Child

*To those who believed in his name, [Jesus] gave
the right to become children of God.*

– John 1:12

Your Adoption Papers

On that special day when you ask Jesus to forgive your sins once and for all, you are adopted into the family of God. Have you done that yet? If not, why not do it today?

If you are part of God's family, fill out the special adoption papers. These papers say you belong to God's family.

Savior & Me
ADOPTION PAPERS

For: _____

Date: _____

Church: _____

How did you find out about Jesus?:
_____
_____

Prayer

Dear God, I am so thankful You adopted me into Your family. Amen.

You Are God's Child

*To those who believed in his name, [Jesus] gave
the right to become children of God.*

– John 1:12

Your Perfect Father

Your Father in heaven is different than your earthly dad. God is perfect. He knows everything you say and do. He loves you perfectly and answers your prayers. Every human has faults, including your parents. God doesn't! Make a list that describes the perfect father. Which of the things on your list are true for God?

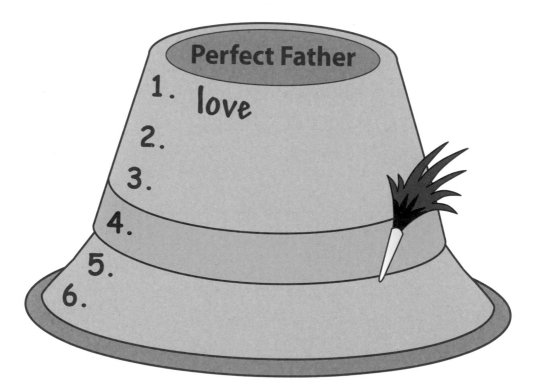

Perfect Father

1. love
2.
3.
4.
5.
6.

Prayer

Father in heaven, thank You for listening to me when I pray. Thank You for caring for me and answering my prayers. I love You! Amen.

You Are God's Child

*To those who believed in his name, [Jesus] gave
the right to become children of God.*

– John 1:12

Praising God

Robin heard her parents talking about their new city mayor.

"Carl Gruber grew up on my street," said Robin's mom. "I've known him for years."

"He's very bright, and he has many good ideas. He can do a lot of things well," Dad said.

Her mom added, "I know he will be helpful to this city as mayor. He is a wonderful man."

Robin's parents were praising the new mayor. The Bible tells of a boy named David who wrote and sang songs that praised God. David's songs, called psalms in the Bible, told people how great and holy God is. Sometimes David's songs were prayers asking God for help.

In Psalm 100, David prays and says God is to be honored: "Worship the LORD with gladness; come before him with joyful songs."

When you worship God when you pray, you say good things about Him and His name.

Your Turn

1. How do you think God feels when you offer praise prayers to Him?
2. How do you feel when you praise and worship Him?

_____

_____

_____

_____

Prayer

Dear Father in heaven, I praise You and worship You. You are perfect and good. Help me remember to keep Your name special. Amen.

You Are God's Child

*To those who believed in his name, [Jesus] gave
the right to become children of God.*

– John 1:12

Praise God's Name Match-Up

God's names tell you how special He is and how you can honor Him.
Look up these Scriptures and draw a line from the Scripture to the correct
description. Pray these names back to God. For example, "God, You are
the Shepherd of Israel."

Psalm 24:7   Shepherd of Israel

Psalm 80:1   Prince of Peace

Isaiah 9:6   King of Glory

Job 37:23   Holy God

2 Corinthians 1:3   Creator

1 Samuel 2:2   God of all Comfort

Isaiah 40:28   The Almighty

Prayer

God, You have many special names, and I want to worship You all the
days of my life. Amen.

You Are God's Child

*To those who believed in his name, [Jesus] gave
the right to become children of God.*

– John 1:12

Kingdom Castle

God wants you in His kingdom. But how do you get into the castle? It's
easy! You just need to pray like this:

*God, I want to be in Your kingdom! I believe Your Son Jesus died on the
cross to pay for my sins. Then He rose from
the dead to give me everlasting life with You.
I give You my life. Amen.*

If you have prayed that prayer, draw your
face in the window of the
castle tower. Draw the faces
of people who know God
in the other windows.
Draw someone who
doesn't know God in
the door, and pray
for him or her
every day.

217

You Are God's Child

To those who believed in his name, [Jesus] gave the right to become children of God.

– John 1:12

Lovable Words

Write something you have heard or read in the Bible that you like. It can be about a person, a story, or something you've learned, such as "God loves me."

Lovable Words Page

Prayer

Dear God, thank You for Your Word. The best fact is that You love me and want me to be Your child. Thank You! Teach me to love Your Word and keep it in my heart. Amen.

God Has Plans for You

"I know the plans I have for you," declares the LORD.
– Jeremiah 29:11

When Plans Fail

Lora's dad had an out-of-town business meeting to attend. Instead of staying behind as they usually did, Lora, her sister, and her mom were going with Dad. Lora was excited! The plan was that Dad would go to his meeting in the morning and take the family to the zoo in the afternoon. Then they would relax by the hotel pool in the evening.

During the long car ride, Lora's sister came down with an earache. So instead of fun at the zoo and the pool, the family spent the day at a hospital. Their plans for a fun afternoon and evening were ruined. But what went right? Lora's family spent time together. They prayed and trusted God to heal Lora's sister. The trip did not go as planned, but it went God's way.

You probably make plans every day. You arrange time with friends for classes and activities. But sometimes your plans don't work out. The only thing you can always depend on is that God's plans never fail. Doing things God's way means you trust that He has something even better for you when your plans fail. God's plans are perfect and for your good.

Your Turn

1. Why should you pray for God's plans to happen?
2. How do you think life on Earth is different from life in heaven?

_____

_____

_____

Prayer

Dear God, help me want the things You want. Show me how to trust Your plans when mine go wrong. Amen.

God Has Plans for You

"I know the plans I have for you," declares the LORD.
– Jeremiah 29:11

My Six Prayers

Practice letting God's plans guide your prayers. Trace each letter of "pray" and talk to God about each area.

PRAY **for help to do good things for others.**

PRAY **for boldness to tell friends about Jesus.**

PRAY **for help in being kind – even to those who are mean.**

PRAY **for help in remembering to read the Bible.**

PRAY **for help in obeying my parents.**

PRAY **that when my plans don't work out, I will trust God's plans.**

God Has Plans for You

"I know the plans I have for you," declares the LORD.
– Jeremiah 29:11

Your Daily Bread

Bread is one of the most basic foods people eat. When Jesus said to pray, "Give us today our daily bread," He was saying, "Ask Me for the things you need" (Matthew 6:11). God doesn't promise to give you everything you want, but He does give you what you need. Put an X over the things you want instead of need. Ask God for the things you need.

Prayer

Dear God, I have everything I need. Thank You for loving me and taking care of me. Amen.

God Has Plans for You

"I know the plans I have for you," declares the LORD.
– Jeremiah 29:11

The Sliver

Haley's father tore down the cedar deck behind their house.

"Stay away from those boards," Haley's mom said to her. "You could get wood slivers in your hands and feet."

Haley didn't obey her mother's warning. "Ouch! Mom, I have a sliver!" Haley stuck out her finger.

Haley's mom removed the sliver and applied healing medicine.

What if Haley was too ashamed to admit not obeying? What if she had let the sliver stay in her finger instead of telling her mom? It could have gone deeper into her skin and become infected. Then Haley might have had to go to the doctor, and the sliver would have been harder to remove. Haley trusted her mom to help her.

Haley's hurt finger is kind of like life. The longer you wait to pray for forgiveness of your sins, the worse you feel. Just like Haley's mom removed the sliver, God takes away your sins and makes you feel better. He is always willing to forgive and heal.

Your Turn

1. What should you do when you do something wrong?
2. How does sin change your friendship with God?

_____

_____

_____

_____

Prayer

Dear God, I know I sometimes do what I want even when it's not right. Please forgive me. Remind me to tell You what I have done wrong right away so You will forgive me. Amen.

God Has Plans for You

"I know the plans I have for you," declares the LORD.
– Jeremiah 29:11

Sliver-Free Fingers

Under the wood with slivers, write some sins people need to tell God. If you have done some of them and asked God for forgiveness, draw a cross on the bandaged finger because God has forgiven you.

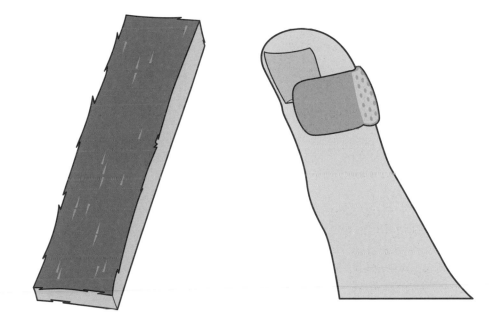

Slivers

_____

_____

_____

Prayer

God, thank You for forgiving me when I sin. Thank You for helping the pain go away. Amen.

God Has Plans for You

"I know the plans I have for you," declares the LORD.
– Jeremiah 29:11

Forgiveness Steps

Figure out each step to forgiveness by filling in the blank letters on each step. Practice using these steps the next time someone hurts you. Draw yourself on the steps.

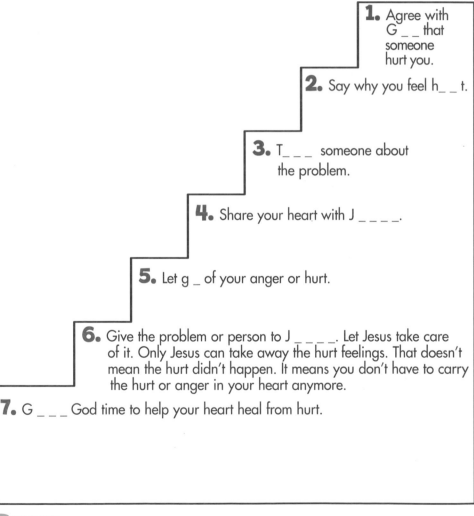

1. Agree with G _ _ that someone hurt you.

2. Say why you feel h_ _ t.

3. T_ _ _ someone about the problem.

4. Share your heart with J _ _ _ _.

5. Let g _ of your anger or hurt.

6. Give the problem or person to J _ _ _ _. Let Jesus take care of it. Only Jesus can take away the hurt feelings. That doesn't mean the hurt didn't happen. It means you don't have to carry the hurt or anger in your heart anymore.

7. G _ _ _ God time to help your heart heal from hurt.

Prayer

Dear God, thank You for being ready to forgive me. Help me be ready to forgive others. Amen.

God Has Plans for You

"I know the plans I have for you," declares the Lord.
– Jeremiah 29:11

Big Temptations

Everyone is tempted to do the wrong thing sometimes. With God's strength and help, you can avoid doing bad things. Draw a line from the temptation on the left to how God will help you on the right.

When I am tempted to...

- Make fun of someone who is different
- Cheat when playing a game
- Laugh at someone being teased
- Use bad words when I'm angry
- Watch TV shows that I'm not supposed to
- Not clean up my room as told
- Push toys under my bed
- Stay outside and play too late

God helps me to...

- be inside on time.
- clean my room.
- watch shows that honor God.
- be kind to others, even if it's hard.
- follow the rules.
- use kind words.
- put them away where they belong.
- stand up for others.

Prayer

Dear Lord, thank You for giving me ways to keep away from temptation. Help me know what keeps me from You so I can ask for Your help. Amen.

Prayer Is Sweet

God has surely listened and has heard my prayer.
– Psalm 66:19

The Berry Bushes

"Look! Berries!" said Kate as she and Nicole hiked in the woods behind their house.

"Let's eat some," Nicole said.

Kate said, "Are you sure they are okay?"

Nicole said, "Yes. Let's try one and see if they are sweet."

Nicole plopped one into her mouth. "These are great!"

Kate piled berries into her pocket. "Grandma likes berries"

"Good idea!" said Nicole. "I love to share sweet things with her."

When you pray, you give something sweet to God. "Gracious words are a honeycomb, sweet to the soul and healing to the bones" (Proverbs 16:24). Prayer is a sweet gift of worship too. Use these words as a sweet offering to God:

Dear God, Your beauty shines everywhere on earth.
You love me so much!
You sent Jesus to be my Friend.
You sent Your Spirit to keep me from missing You and Jesus.
You are full of love, and You love me even when I do bad.
You take my sins away and let me start again.
I want to tell you thank You and tell you that I love You!

Your Turn

1. What do you love to eat that is sweet?
2. Name someone who needs your sweet prayers. Pray for that person.

_____

_____

_____

Prayer Is Sweet

God has surely listened and has heard my prayer.
– Psalm 66:19

Berry Bush Puzzle

Can you find and circle the words "Sweet Prayers" hidden in the berry bush?

Prayer

Dear God, I love to pray because I know You listen and respond. Thank You. Amen.

Prayer Is Sweet

God has surely listened and has heard my prayer.
– Psalm 66:19

The Lord's Prayer

Jesus gave people a wonderful way to pray. Many people call it the "Lord's Prayer," and you can find it in Matthew 6:9-13. Read the Lord's prayer in the correct order. Then color the word "pray." For fun, use the color key to create a beautiful picture. Remember, God enjoys hearing you pray.

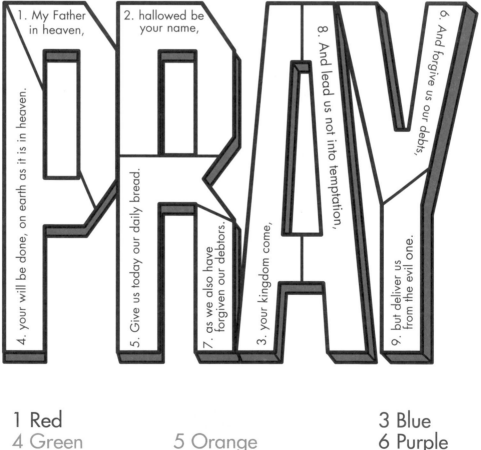

1. My Father in heaven,
2. hallowed be your name,
3. your kingdom come,
4. your will be done, on earth as it is in heaven.
5. Give us today our daily bread.
6. And forgive us our debts,
7. as we also have forgiven our debtors.
8. And lead us not into temptation,
9. but deliver us from the evil one.

1 Red		3 Blue
4 Green	5 Orange	6 Purple
7 Pink	8 Your choice!	9 Brown

Prayer Is Sweet

God has surely listened and has heard my prayer.
– Psalm 66:19

Prayer Breath

Tiffany's dad blew up ten balloons for her birthday party.

"The more you blow, the bigger the balloon gets," Tiffany said. The larger the balloon grew, the more out of breath her dad became.

Mary had the flu. The doctor told her to take three deep breaths as he listened to her lungs. "Her breathing is good," he told her parents.

Ashley's team ran laps on the track. After the first lap, Ashley said, "I'm out of breath."

Taking air into your lungs and letting it out is called "breathing." Breathing is something you do without thinking. That's the way prayer should be too. Just like when you blow up a balloon, the more often you pray, the bigger your faith gets for God. Psalm 150:6 says, "Let everything that has breath praise the LORD."

Praying was like breathing to Jesus. He prayed for the sick and hurting. Jesus saw people who needed prayer everywhere He went. He prayed all of the time for them.

Let prayer become like breathing for you. Make every breath a prayer of praise or a prayer for someone in need (including you).

Your Turn

1. How is praying like breathing for Jesus?
2. What do you see around you that can become a reason for prayer?

_____

_____

_____

_____

Prayer

Dear God, teach me to pray like I breathe. Let me pray as a natural part of living. Show me people who need prayer. Amen.

Prayer Is Sweet

God has surely listened and has heard my prayer.
– Psalm 66:19

The Breathing Prayer

Write the names of people you can pray for in the girl's breath. Pray for these people every day.

Prayer

Dear God, I want praying to be automatic so I can talk to You all the time. Amen.

Prayer Is Sweet

God has surely listened and has heard my prayer.
– Psalm 66:19

Prayer Partner

Write the name of an older girl or woman you love and are comfortable with. Ask her if she will pray with you once a week.

FROM: TO:
SUBJECT:

Hello...

Prayer

Dear God, I thank You for letting me talk to You and know You. Although I can't see You, I know You exist and You love me. You are the one and only true God. You fill my heart with comfort and joy. Amen.

Prayer Is Sweet

God has surely listened and has heard my prayer.
– Psalm 66:19

Prayer Squares

Look at the prayer squares. Finish coloring each square. Pray for what the square shows.

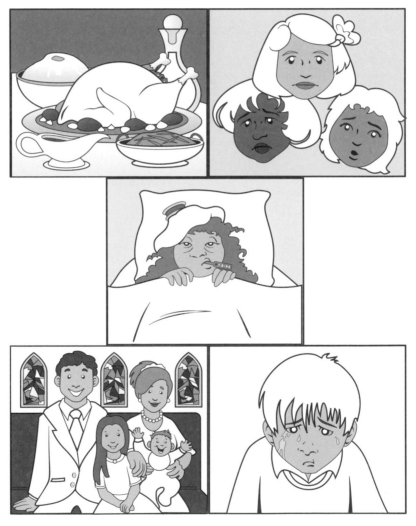

Prayer

Thank You, God, that I take joy in praying. Teach me to enjoy the things You enjoy. I want to pray with Your joy. Amen.

Getting Close to God

I will sing to the LORD all my life.
– Psalm 104:33

Backyard Prayers

Megan was having a sleepover with her friends Ashley, Paige, and Rachel. Megan had planned activities. After some games, they'd watch a movie and eat popcorn. Then they'd pray together.

But things didn't work out. One by one, the girls fell asleep. Disappointed, Megan prayed by herself.

"That sounds like Jesus," Megan's mom said the next day after Megan told her what happened. "And you weren't alone. Jesus was with you!"

"What do you mean?" asked Megan.

"Jesus and His friends were at Gethsemane," said Mom. " 'Sit here while I go over there and pray,' Jesus told the guys. He took Peter, James, and John deeper into the garden. 'Stay here and keep watch with me,' Jesus said. Then He moved a little bit away to pray. When He went back, Peter, James, and John were sleeping. 'Couldn't you men keep watch with me for one hour?' Jesus asked Peter. Then Jesus went away a second time to pray. The same thing happened. And then it happened again.' "

"That does sound like my friends," said Megan. "At least I know Jesus is always with me."

Your Turn

1. What does it mean to be a friend?
2. How do you think Jesus felt when He found His friends sleeping?

_____

_____

_____

Prayer

Dear Jesus, I love You. Thank You for always being with me. Amen.

Getting Close to God

I will sing to the LORD all my life.
– Psalm 104:33

Sleepover Prayer Snacks

Write a short prayer in the center of the girls' popcorn bowl.

Prayer

Dear Jesus, when I pray I'm talking to my Best Friend. I am glad You hear my prayers. Amen.

Getting Close to God

*I will sing to the L*ORD *all my life.*
– Psalm 104:33

Heart Song

Write the name of your favorite worship song on the screen. Pray to God by singing the song directly to Him.

Prayer

Thank You, dear LORD, for music and Your wonderful love. You put songs in my heart. I love to sing prayers to You. Amen.

Getting Close to God

I will sing to the LORD all my life.
– Psalm 104:33

Humpty Dumpty

Jessica felt like she had a big crack in her heart. "Why did my daddy have to leave?" she asked her grandma.

Grandma gave Jessica a big hug. "I know you feel very sad, and crying is normal and healing. Honey, you'll feel better in time. Right now your heart is broken because of your parents' divorce. A broken heart will heal, but it takes time. I'll be here to listen to you any time you need me. Remember the rhyme 'Humpty Dumpty'?"

"Yes," said Jessica looking at Grandma.

Grandma and Jessica said the rhyme together. Grandma smiled as she wrapped her arms around her granddaughter. "Jesus is the only One who can put Humpty Dumpty back together again. Jesus is the only One who can put your broken heart together again."

Grandma brushed Jessica's hair back behind her ears. "The Bible says He will never leave you or forsake you. This divorce wasn't your fault, honey. Give your hurt to God, and in time you will heal."

"Can we pray now?" asked Jessica.

"Sure," said Grandma. "We'll pray together as much as you want."

Your Turn

1. Who can put your broken heart together again?

_____

_____

_____

_____

Prayer

Dear Jesus, I give You my hurts today. When I am feeling alone, help me remember You love me. Amen.

Getting Close to God

I will sing to the LORD all my life.
– Psalm 104:33

Humpty Dumpty's Wall

Look up the Bible story listed on Humpty Dumpty's wall. Read the story about the prodigal son aloud with someone—perhaps your parents—so you can talk about it when you're done.

What caused the people in the story to feel hurt? What happened to take away their hurt?

Now have fun coloring Humpty.

LUKE 15:11-32

Prayer

Dear Jesus, I don't want to be like the boy in the story. I want to always stay connected to You. Amen.

Getting Close to God

I will sing to the LORD all my life.
– Psalm 104:33

Bad News Prayer Boat

Have you experienced bad news? Have you had bad days? God wants to help! Ask God for help and comfort as you finish coloring the boat. Ask God to bring good out of the bad.

Prayer

Thank You, Jesus, for answering my prayers. You are kind and full of mercy. You can turn a bad day into a good one. Amen.

Getting Close to God

*I will sing to the L*ORD *all my life.*
– Psalm 104:33

In Jesus' Name

When you take a note to school from your parents, the teacher accepts it because your mom or dad signed it. The note is sent in your parent's name. In a similar way, Jesus has given you the gift of praying in His name. He said, "You may ask me for anything in my name, and I will do it." Write a prayer on the stationery and end it with, "In Jesus' name. Amen."

Prayer

LORD Jesus, thank You for letting me pray in Your name. Your name is powerful! Amen.

239

God Answers

I waited patiently for the LORD; he turned to me and heard my cry.
– Psalm 40:1

Wait, Wait, Wait

Do you get tired of waiting for your birthday? Do you get tired of waiting for a friend to come out and play? Waiting for your parents to answer questions can take time too. It's hard to wait when you really want something. Sometimes people ask God to hurry up, but He is never in a hurry. He wants what's best when the time is right.

Jennifer's friend didn't know Jesus. Jennifer prayed that Kelly would come to know Him. She prayed for one whole year. One day, God answered, and Kelly came to know Jesus. Jennifer was glad she had never given up.

After she moved, Kim prayed for God to give her a friend. God answered. One week later, she met her new friend, Ruth.

Lauren prayed when her cat was lost. She prayed for three weeks. Then one day she heard Patches meowing at the back door.

Sometimes God holds off on His answers so you will know He is in charge. Other times He waits so you will pray more. God also says no at times because He always knows what is best.

Your Turn

1. When have you had to wait for God to answer your prayers?
2. Name two people in the Bible who waited for God's answer.

_____

_____

_____

Prayer

Dear God, give me patience and trust as I wait for Your answers to my prayers. Amen.

God Answers

I waited patiently for the LORD; he turned to me and heard my cry.
– Psalm 40:1

Clock Talk

Create the face of the clock. Write in the numbers, and make the hands. Let the clock remind you that sometimes you must wait for God to answer your prayers.

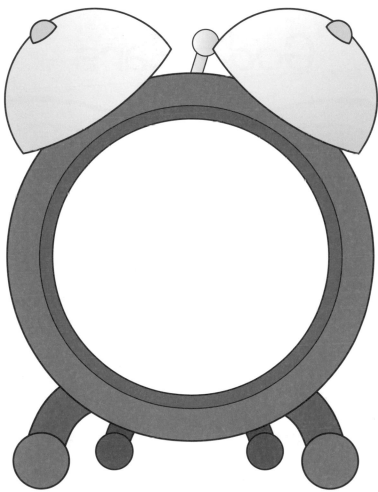

Prayer

Dear LORD, when I pray and it seems like You don't answer, I know I just need to be patient because You always hear me. Amen.

God Answers

I waited patiently for the LORD; he turned to me and heard my cry.
– Psalm 40:1

Full Ears

God cares about you. He wants you to share everything, including the things you are afraid of. Fill God's ears with your troubles and ask God to help you. Keep praying while you wait for His answers.

God's Ears

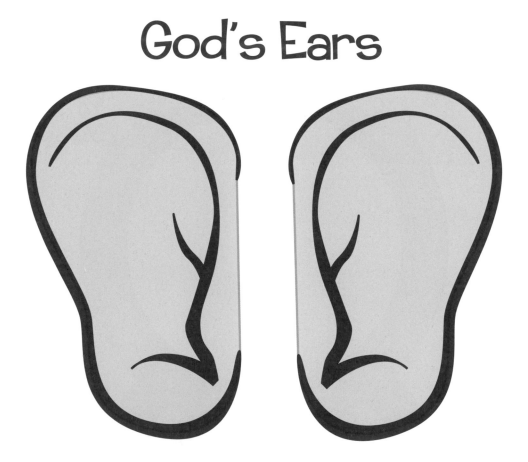

Prayer

Dear God, thank You for helping me with my troubles. I thank You for always being ready to talk with me. Amen.

God Answers

I waited patiently for the LORD; he turned to me and heard my cry.
– Psalm 40:1

Flying Free

Haley's mom asked her to empty the dishwasher.

"Later. I'm in the middle of something important," Haley replied.

Haley's mom had never heard her daughter answer in such a way. But Mom knew where it came from. Haley had just returned from a weeklong visit with her cousins. Her cousins didn't speak respectfully to their parents. Also, Haley had mentioned that she didn't talk to God while she was away. She was too busy swimming and hiking with her cousins.

Praying—talking to God—is important. When you allow yourself to get too worried or too busy, you don't pray. And that leads to bad things. God wants you to fly free from bad thinking.

People tend to think like those around them. When you hang around people with negative attitudes, that rubs off on you. And it's the same with ungodly music, books, and movies. Your thinking will change. Prayer helps your mind stay clear and clean and focused on God.

When you pray, you learn to think right and do right. Prayer helps you soar to new heights with God.

Your Turn

1. What are some things that might keep you from praying?
2. Write down one thing that helps you remember to pray.

_____

_____

_____

Prayer

Dear God, help me keep my mind focused on You. Clean my mind as I talk to You. I confess I have let myself think bad thoughts. I want my mind to be filled with Your peace. Amen.

God Answers

I waited patiently for the LORD; he turned to me and heard my cry.
– Psalm 40:1

Flying Girl Maze

Follow the girl as she prays and gets past obstacles to good thinking. Help her focus on God.

Prayer

Dear LORD, teach me through Your Word to think and act more like You do. I want my mind to be filled with Your truths. Amen.

God Answers

I waited patiently for the LORD; he turned to me and heard my cry.
– Psalm 40:1

Your Scary List

Make a list of things that scare you. Make another list of what you can do to take away your fears. You can draw pictures or use words.

Things That Scare me...

Take-away List

Prayer

Dear God, remind me to turn to You in prayer when I am afraid. I know You will hear me and comfort me. Amen.

245

God Answers

I waited patiently for the LORD; he turned to me and heard my cry.
– Psalm 40:1

Fanned Flames

Have you ever helped build a campfire? Gently fanning the flames helped
the fire to grow. In the same way, we pray to "fan the flames" of our faith.
Color the fire. Then finish the prayer starters.

God, I pray my family will...

I pray You will help me...

Dear God, teach me...

Dear God, help me to...

Prayer

Dear God, please fan the flames of my heart to want to pray more. There
are so many things I can pray about. Amen.

Growing Your Prayer Life

The LORD...hears the prayer of the righteous.
– Proverbs 15:29

Step Up

When it is time for us to do something better, people might say, "It's time to step up. So let's step up and become persistent in praying. To "persist" means to keep doing something again and again. When we pray persistently, we keep praying and don't give up. Step up—don't give up!

The Bible says you "should always pray and not give up" (Luke 18:1). Sometimes when life gets hard, you might pray for a while, but soon stop. You might think your prayers aren't being heard. God hears each and every prayer. He likes it when you persist in prayer. He will answer.

Jesus told His disciples a story to teach them to persist in prayer. A widow went to see a judge. Her enemies kept bothering her. She wanted the judge to do something about it. Over and over, the judge said no. The widow didn't stop asking. She went back to the judge many times.

Then one day the judge said, "Because this widow has been so persistent, I will see that she is treated fairly."

Jesus explained to His disciples that God hears those who pray to Him. He will see that they get what they need. Don't give up—step up! Keep on praying!

Your Turn

1. What made the widow so persistent with the judge?
2. What keeps you going back to God in prayer?

_____

_____

_____

Prayer

Dear God, thank You that I can come to You over and over again. You never get tired of me! I will step up and persist in prayer. Amen.

Growing Your Prayer Life

The LORD…hears the prayer of the righteous.

– Proverbs 15:29

Prayer Steps

Write some prayers on the steps, and then pray them. Be persistent. Note God's answers on this page too.

1. _____

_____

_____

2. _____

_____

_____

_____

3. _____

_____

_____

_____

Prayer

Dear God, I am happy I can come to You in prayer anytime I need or want to. Your answers are always perfect. Amen.

Growing Your Prayer Life

The LORD...hears the prayer of the righteous.
– Proverbs 15:29

My Prayer Mural

Do you enjoy painting or drawing? Painting and praying have some things in common. They please the person doing them, and they please the receiver. God enjoys your prayers. Paint a picture of your prayer on the wall.

Prayer

Dear God, thank You for loving and understanding my prayers whether I paint them or say them. Amen.

Growing Your Prayer Life

The LORD…hears the prayer of the righteous.
— **Proverbs 15:29**

Stones of the Past

Dana's dad was a stone mason. He knew how to cut and shape big rocks to make them fit together. Sometimes he turned rocks into animal shapes. Dana loved to watch her dad work—he used all kinds of tools. Bits of stone flew everywhere! So she didn't get too close!

Dad was telling Dana about stones while they ate lunch.

"In Bible times, small stones were used as weapons. David picked up five stones to fight the giant Goliath and kill him." Dad took a sip of lemonade. "Bible-time people sharpened stones into knives. Larger stones were shaped to cover wells and mouths of caves. Stones were stacked to form altars to honor God."

"Didn't God write in stone?" asked Dana.

"Yes! He wrote the Ten Commandments in stone for Moses."

"Wow!" said Dana. "I would like to write in stone."

Dad took his hammer and pick from his backpack. "Let's make a heart." As they worked, Dad said, "Our prayers are like stone. They stay with God forever."

"Let's write, 'I love You, God!' " Dana said.

As they worked, Dad said, "Our prayers are like stone. They stay with God forever."

Your Turn

1. What did you learn about stones?
2. What would you like to write in stone for God to remember?

_____

_____

Prayer

Dear God, thank You for listening to my prayers and remembering them forever. I am glad You answer them. Amen.

Growing Your Prayer Life

The LORD...hears the prayer of the righteous.

– Proverbs 15:29

My Prayer Stone

Create your own prayer stone. "Chisel" two things you want to tell God in prayer.

Prayer

Dear God, thank You for answering my prayers and loving me. Amen.

Growing Your Prayer Life

The Lord...hears the prayer of the righteous.
– Proverbs 15:29

A Prayer Wall

Castle walls are made of stone. Write your name at the top of the wall. Now write the names of people you love. Write down your neighbors' names too. Pray these people will know and love God more every day.

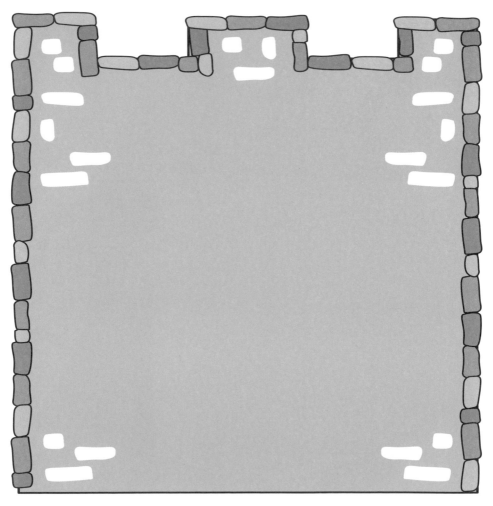

Prayer

Dear God, help me pray for the people around me...and for me...that we will grow in You every day. Amen.

Growing Your Prayer Life

The Lord...hears the prayer of the righteous.
– Proverbs 15:29

A Dancer's Prayers

Karla loved to dance. She told her mom, "I like to pray when I dance. I pray that people will discover how much God loves them." Write a prayer for each of these dance steps.

Prayer

Dear Jesus, I am glad You will meet with me anyplace and anytime. Help me never brag about praying. Amen.

Seeking God's Purpose

Ask and it will be given to you; seek and you will find.
– Matthew 7:7

The Dog Bone

Suzie had a little dog named Cleo, who loved doggy bones. Suzie would hide bones in the yard and watch Cleo search for them. Suzie especially loved watching Cleo sniff by the fence posts, deck, and bushes for the bone. Once she found where a bone was hidden, she would wag her tail and happily dig for it. Suzie wanted to meet Cleo's needs, but she also wanted Cleo to exercise her body and mind.

God wants to give you what you need, but sometimes He wants you to work for it. Jesus said, "Seek and you will find" (Matthew 7:7). To "seek" means to look for something. Jesus was saying you should seek what God has for you. Praying is kind of like working for what you need. God's plan is for you to know Him, but He wants you to read the Bible and pray to dig up the truths of God. You grow and remember better when you have to work.

Love, forgiveness, and joy are what you find when you dig into God's Word. When you pray, you find answers to your questions.

Your Turn

1. Why do you think God wants you to seek Him?
2. Where do you think you should hunt for more knowledge about God?

_____

_____

_____

_____

Prayer

Dear Jesus, I am glad You want me to grow in You and be spiritually fit. Keep my mind and heart eager to seek You.

Seeking God's Purpose

Ask and it will be given to you; seek and you will find.
– Matthew 7:7

A People Bone

Dig up the good things of God. Circle the bones that will help you find God's best for you.

Prayer

Dear God, give me a hunger for Your Word and a willingness to obey You. Amen.

255

Seeking God's Purpose

Ask and it will be given to you; seek and you will find.
– Matthew 7:7

Stop, Drop, and Roll Chart

What do you do if your clothes catch on fire? You stop, drop to the ground, and roll to put the flames out. That works for prayer too. When you have difficulty, God wants you to stop and drop to your knees to pray. Then you are rolling your troubles onto God. He will take care of you. If you are with people, you can stop, drop, and roll in your mind.

Create a stop, drop, and roll chart. Under the stop picture, write today's date. Under the drop picture, write today's verse or a Scripture you like. Under the roll picture, write your prayer request to God. You can make this chart every time you need to work through a problems.

_____   _____   _____

_____   _____   _____

_____   _____   _____

_____   _____   _____

Prayer

Dear God, help me remember to pray instead of complain. I want to be thankful for everything You have given me. Amen.

Seeking God's Purpose

Ask and it will be given to you; seek and you will find.
– Matthew 7:7

Prayer Walk

After delivering His people from slavery, God promised them a new home in a different country. He told Joshua, the leader of the Israelites, "Get ready to cross the Jordan River into the land I am about to give to... the Israelites. I will give you every place where you set your foot." God told His people to be strong and brave. "Be careful to obey all the law my servant Moses gave you...then you will be prosperous and successful" (Joshua 1).

You also can dedicate to God the places where you set your feet: your school, your home, your playground, your church. As your feet take you to these places, you can pray. Pray the kids in your class will know Jesus. Pray your teacher will love God and teach you good things. Pray your family will seek God's guidance and live for Him. Pray as you slide, swing, and climb. Walk from one end of the playground to the other asking God to protect the kids. Pray the leaders at your church follow God with all their hearts.

Let your feet and heart walk for God.

Your Turn

1. Why do you think God gave His people, the Israelites, land?
2. Where do you walk each day? Do you pray for the people you see?

_____

_____

_____

_____

Prayer

Dear God, thank You for the promises You give me. Help me dedicate my school, my home, my church, and the places I play to You. Amen.

Seeking God's Purpose

Ask and it will be given to you; seek and you will find.
– Matthew 7:7

Your Prayer Area

Draw your prayer area. In the boxes along the street, draw the places you go. Remember to pray everywhere you go.

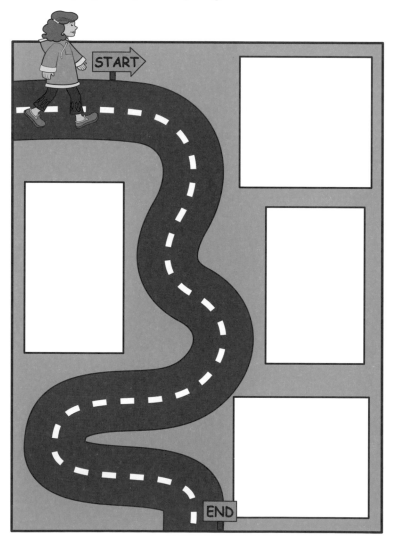

Prayer

Dear God, when I am walking, please remind me to pray for the people I pass by. Amen.

Seeking God's Purpose

Ask and it will be given to you; seek and you will find.
– Matthew 7:7

Creative Prayer Snapshots

Look at the prayer pictures in the boxes. Write below each one what you might pray when you do that activity. For the last box, draw an activity you do and can use as a prayer time.

_____   _____   _____

_____   _____

Prayer

Thank You, God, for loving me and wanting to talk to me. Give me creative ideas for praying each day. Help me make prayer a habit. Amen.

Seeking God's Purpose

Ask and it will be given to you; seek and you will find.
– Matthew 7:7

Zacchaeus and Jesus

Zacchaeus was a short Jewish man who collected taxes for the invading Romans. He cheated his people often to get more money for himself. When he heard Jesus was coming, Zacchaeus climbed a tree to see Him. Jesus saw him, talked to him, and forgave him. Draw your way through the maze to help Zacchaeus reach Jesus.

Prayer

Dear Jesus, help me always seek Your love and guidance. I want to serve You completely. Amen.

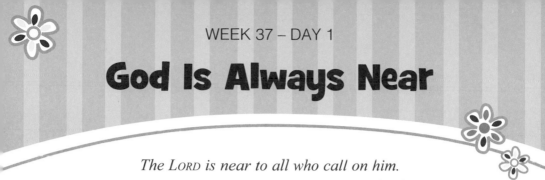

God Is Always Near

The LORD is near to all who call on him.

– Psalm 145:18

Rosa's Bad Dream

Rosa's family had just moved into their new house. One afternoon, the neighbor's dog barged in through the front door, growling and baring his teeth at Rosa. Rosa ran to the end of the hallway, the dog snapping at her heels.

"Daddy!" she screamed. "Help! The dog is trying to hurt me!"

Rosa felt strong arms around her. She blinked, looked up, and saw she wasn't in the hallway at all. Instead, she was in her bed in her new bedroom. Her father sat next to her with a reassuring smile on his face. The dog was nowhere in sight.

"You had a bad dream," explained Rosa's father. "It was easy for me to hear you call out in our new house because my room is right across the hallway."

Rosa felt calmer. "It's good to know you are so close. I'm glad my bedroom isn't in the basement."

Rosa's father heard her cry out because he was nearby. God is near you no matter where you are, even if you are in a new town, a new house, a new church. Everywhere you go, God is with you.

Your Turn

1. How does it feel to call out and have someone answer quickly?
2. Why does God want you to know He is always near you?

_____

_____

_____

_____

Prayer

God, I am so thankful You are always near me. Amen.

God Is Always Near

The LORD is near to all who call on him.

– Psalm 145:18

A Special Place

Draw a picture of yourself in an unusual place in your house. Go to that special place, call out to God, and thank Him for being near you wherever you are.

Prayer

Dear God, thank You for always being near me. When I remember that, I don't need to be afraid. Amen.

God Is Always Near

The LORD is near to all who call on him.

– Psalm 145:18

Prayer Partners

On each finger of the praying hands, write the name of someone you can pray with. The next time you are with those people, join in their prayers or ask them to pray with you.

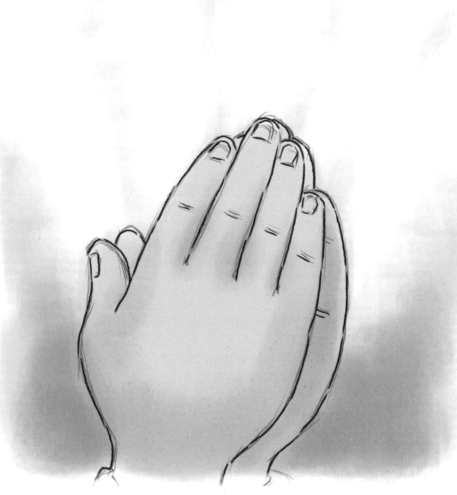

Prayer

Dear LORD, thank You for the people You put in my life who will encourage me to pray. Amen.

God Is Always Near

The LORD *is near to all who call on him.*
– Psalm 145:18

A Good Friend

Beth liked talking with Mr. Browne, the music teacher. He'd heard her singing in music class and told her she had a good voice.

One day, Beth noticed that Mr. Browne wore an ankle cast. "I'm sorry you hurt your ankle," she said. "What happened?" She listened as he explained how he'd tripped on the stairs.

"Thank you, Beth, for asking about my ankle," he said. "You are a good friend. You talk and listen."

A good friend. Beth smiled. She liked that.

Beth learned something very important: Friends talk with each other and listen to each other.

Jesus talked to His disciples and followers about God and told them everything He could. He also listened to them. He was a good friend.

You can talk to Jesus when you pray; He always listens. Jesus will talk to you too. He'll tell you everything He can about God. You can listen to Jesus in your heart and when you read the Bible. He's your Friend.

Your Turn

1. List some friends you can talk to and who will talk and listen in return.
2. Good friends talk about things on their minds. Name one thing you'd like to talk about with a good friend right now.

_____

_____

_____

Prayer

Jesus, I am so glad I can talk to You and that You listen and talk with me. Thank You for letting me talk about anything on my mind. Amen.

God Is Always Near

The LORD is near to all who call on him.

– Psalm 145:18

Talk and Listen to Jesus

You can talk and listen to Jesus anytime, any place. Draw a picture of yourself next to Him.

Prayer

Dear Jesus, I am so glad You are my Friend. I know when I call out to You, You will hear me and respond. Amen.

God Is Always Near

The LORD is near to all who call on him.

– Psalm 145:18

Prayer Bookmark

Make this bookmark to remind you about Jesus' prayer example.

What You Need
- Ruler
- Pencil
- Scissors
- Markers
- Construction paper or card stock

What to Do

Measure and cut a piece of construction paper or card stock 2 inches wide by 8 inches long.

Write, "LORD, teach me to pray!" on the bookmark. Decorate the bookmark with a border, hearts, and other designs. Use your prayer bookmark to keep your place in this book or in your Bible.

Prayer

Dear LORD, teach me to pray. I want to honor You. Amen.

God Is Always Near

The LORD is near to all who call on him.

– Psalm 145:18

God Listens All the Time

God promises to listen to you anytime, anywhere. List different places you go during your day. Use your list to help you remember to talk to God at different times and places.

Prayer

Dear LORD, thank You for keeping Your promise to listen to me. I'm glad You are my Friend. Amen.

Getting a Clean Heart

Search me, God, and know my heart.
– Psalm 139:23

Test Your Heart

Stacey's parents were planning a birthday party for a child at the local mission. The little girl's father was out of work, and the family had lost their home.

"Let me help with the party," begged Stacey. "I like going to the mission." Stacey wanted to help with the party, but she also hoped she would get a gift too. She looked forward to eating cake and ice cream. She prayed she could go, but her reasons were partly selfish.

Alexandra's family prayed often. She was comfortable praying out loud, so Sunday-school teachers often called on her to pray in class. Her classmates thought of Alexandra as a prayer leader.

"God, I pray that kids everywhere will come to know You as Lord and Savior," Alexandra prayed. "I thank You that the kids in this Sunday-school class know You. I'm glad we aren't in darkness like other kids." Alexandra liked being the center of attention. She prayed for the wrong reason.

Remember to check your heart before you pray. God wants you to talk to Him because you love Him and He loves you. He wants you to pray with a heart toward Him, not toward yourself.

Your Turn

1. How were Stacey and Alexandria alike?
2. What can you do before you pray to be sure your heart is pure?

_____

_____

_____

Prayer

Dear God, please search my heart. Show me my selfishness before I pray. Help me to know what You want me to pray for. Amen.

Getting a Clean Heart

Search me, God, and know my heart.

– Psalm 139:23

My Heart Test

Before you pray, ask *why* you are praying. Is your heart pure? Solve the puzzle to discover an important prayer reminder.

A	B	C	D	E	F	G	H	I	J	K	L	M
1	2	3	4	5	6	7	8	9	10	11	12	13

N	O	P	Q	R	S	T	U	V	W	X	Y	Z
14	15	16	17	18	19	20	21	22	23	24	25	26

___ ___ ___ ___
16 18   1   25

___ ___ ___
 6   15 18

___ ___ ___
20   8   5

___ ___ ___ ___ ___
18   9   7   8   20

___ ___ ___ ___ ___ ___ ___
18   5   1   19 15 14 19

Prayer

Dear God, I want to pray with a right heart. Amen.

Getting a Clean Heart

Search me, God, and know my heart.
– Psalm 139:23

Pray or Complain

"Sing and make music from your heart to the LORD, always giving thanks to God the Father for everything, in the name of our LORD Jesus Christ" (Ephesians 5:19-20). Do you have a thankful heart and attitude? Make a list of things you complain about inside the frowning, complaining mouth. Write "Thank You, God" inside the happy, praying mouth. Which mouth pleases Jesus?

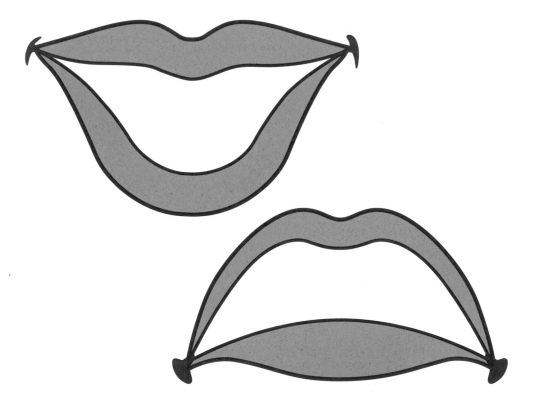

Prayer

Dear God, help me remember to talk to You before I complain. I want to be thankful for all I have. Amen.

Getting a Clean Heart

Search me, God, and know my heart.
– Psalm 139:23

Danielle Leaves a Message

Danielle looked outside. It was a rainy, dreary Saturday morning.

"Would you like to call Angie to see if she can come over today to play?" Danielle's mother asked.

Danielle nodded eagerly. She reached for the phone and called Angie. The phone range one…two…three…four…five times. Then Danielle heard a voice. *Is it Angie?*

"We can't come to the phone right now. Please leave a message after the tone, and we'll return your call." Then the machine beeped. Danielle spoke clearly into the phone, giving her name and number so Angie could call her back. She hung up in disappointment.

When you telephone or text a friend, you may connect or you you may have to leave a message and wait. God never asks you to leave a message. That's why Jeremiah 33:3 is sometimes referred to as "God's Telephone Number": "Call to me and I will answer you."

Your Turn

1. Why did Danielle feel disappointed?
2. Have you ever been disappointed when a friend didn't answer the phone? Why?
3. Why is God's promise in Jeremiah 33:3 so special?

_____

_____

_____

_____

Prayer

Dear God, thank You for always being here, always listening, and always answering when I call. Amen.

Getting a Clean Heart

Search me, God, and know my heart.
– Psalm 139:23

My Contacts

Fill in the phone numbers of your family and friends. Be sure to write down God's number first: Jeremiah 33:3.

Prayer

Dear God, thank You for Your promise to always answer my prayers. Amen.

Getting a Clean Heart

Search me, God, and know my heart.
– Psalm 139:23

God's Nudges

Sometimes God gives nudges—little thoughts to remind you to pray. Jessie saw a little girl in a wheelchair with both legs in casts. Remembering how much she enjoyed soccer, Jessie silently prayed, *Thank You, God, for my good legs. Help the girl in the wheelchair be healthy and happy.* Name some nudges you might get from God during your day. Write down what you might pray.

Prayer

L ORD, I'm listening for Your nudges today. Help me hear You. Amen.

Getting a Clean Heart

Search me, God, and know my heart.

– Psalm 139:23

One Way to Practice Praying

God wants you to pray, but it can be hard to keep praying every day. Prayer takes practice. Solve the puzzle to find out what 1 Thessalonians 5:17 says.

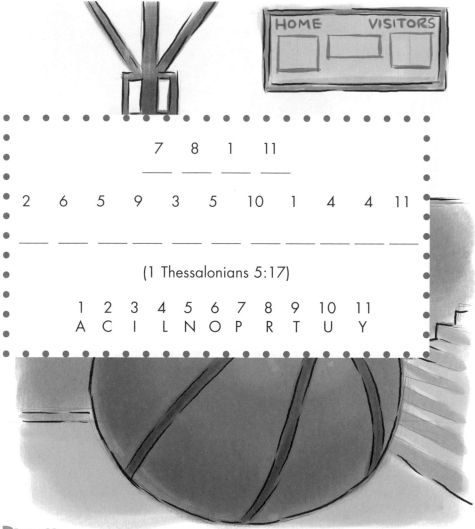

```
      7   8   1   11
     ___ ___ ___ ___

 2   6   5   9   3   5   10   1   4   4   11
___ ___ ___ ___ ___ ___ ___ ___ ___ ___ ___

           (1 Thessalonians 5:17)

     1  2  3  4  5  6  7  8  9  10  11
     A  C  I  L  N  O  P  R  T   U   Y
```

Prayer

LORD, I want to know You and be close to You. Help me keep praying. Amen.

Your Heavenly Father

*[God said,] "I will be a Father to you, and
you will be my sons and daughters."*

– 2 Corinthians 6:18

A Father's Love

Have your parents ever told you that you light up their lives? Have your grandparents told you that you are their sunshine? Even when they are having a bad day, you bring them joy.

God knows it can be hard to understand Him all the time. He knows you are not perfect and that you make mistakes. He loves you just as you are…and always will. He is the perfect parent. He is your heavenly Father, and He watches over you.

God wants you to understand His love for you, so He compares Himself to a father. A father's love is an idea that you recognize. Like a good father, God gives you life, cares for you, and protects you. God is more than good though. He is perfect. He is your loving, powerful, merciful heavenly Father who loves you.

Your Turn

1. Why does God compare Himself to a father?
2. List some ways God shows you perfect Fatherly love.

_____

_____

_____

_____

Prayer

Father God, I love You. Thank You for giving me life, caring for me, and protecting me. Amen.

Your Heavenly Father

*[God said,] "I will be a Father to you, and
you will be my sons and daughters."*

– 2 Corinthians 6:18

God's Fatherly Love

How does God show you love like a perfect Father? Make a list in the sun.

Prayer

Dear God, thank You for being my heavenly Father. I am so glad You
are with me now and forever. Amen.

Your Heavenly Father

*[God said,] "I will be a Father to you, and
you will be my sons and daughters."*

– 2 Corinthians 6:18

Your Birthday!

Did you know God planned for you to be born? He created you using
your father and mother. He designed your gifts and talents. The day you
were born was a very special day! Fill in the blanks to record what God
considered on your special day. Have your parents help you. When you
are done, make a copy and hang it on your wall.

To Be Born:_____
(your name)

Date:_____
(your birthdate)

Time:_____
(your time of birth)

Place:_____
(where you were born)

Weather:_____
(conditions on that day)

Other Events:_____
*(other events in your family, community, nation,
and world going on that day)*

Prayer

Dear Father God, thank You for creating me and planning my life. I love
You, and I love Mom and Dad. Amen.

God's Awesome Word

*[God said,] "I will be a Father to you, and
you will be my sons and daughters."*

– 2 Corinthians 6:18

God Loves You!

Sharise and her father played a special game every night when they prayed together at bedtime. "How much do you love me, Daddy?" she always asked. "Do you love me this much?" Sharise pressed together her thumb and index finger, and then opened them a little bit.

"No, I love you much more than that!" Sharise's dad always answered and smiled. "I love you this much!" He would spread his arms out as wide as he could.

God's fatherly love for you is even bigger! In fact, the Bible says His love is hard for us to imagine. God's love surpasses knowledge (Ephesians 3:19). God's love for you is bigger, greater, wider, longer, higher, and deeper than any other love. He wants you to feel His big, big love so you can be close to Him, know Him better, and walk with Him every day.

Your Turn

1. What is something that reminds you of God's love for you?
2. What helps you stay close to God and grow in Him?

_____

_____

_____

_____

Prayer

Heavenly Father, thank You for Your big, big love. I love You back. Amen.

Your Heavenly Father

[God said,] "I will be a Father to you, and you will be my sons and daughters."

– 2 Corinthians 6:18

How Big Is God's Love?

God planned long ago to spend time with you now. His invitation to you is found in the Bible. Fill in the blanks to see how much God love you.

Wider than _____
(name the largest field or park you know)

Longer than _____
(name the longest road or street you know)

Higher than _____
(name the highest building or mountain you know)

Deeper than _____
(name the deepest river or lake you know)

Prayer

Heavenly Father, I feel safe and secure when I think about how much You love me. Your love is huge. Thank You. Amen.

Your Heavenly Father

*[God said,] "I will be a Father to you, and
you will be my sons and daughters."*

– 2 Corinthians 6:18

"Care 4 U" Bandages

When you fall and hurt your knee, it feels good when someone asks how you are, helps you up, and offers to put a Band-Aid on your wound. God cares even more! Decorate the two plain Band-Aids. Then create your own bandages that show how much God cares for you.

Prayer

Father God, I know I'm never alone. You love me, and You care about me. Remind me to look to You for help and comfort. Amen.

Your Heavenly Father

*[God said,] "I will be a Father to you, and
you will be my sons and daughters."*

– 2 Corinthians 6:18

God's Hands of Power

God's hands are powerful enough to shake the earth, yet gentle enough to comfort you when you are hurting. The Bible talks about God's hands to help us think about His power. Draw a line from each verse to the picture you think best fits.

With [the LORD] at my right hand, I will not be shaken.
~ Psalm 16:8

Show me the wonders of your great love, you who save by your right hand. ~ Psalm 17:7

Save us and help us with your right hand. ~ Psalm 60:5

Prayer

Heavenly Father, Your hands help me, strengthen me, and steady me. You are amazing. Amen.

God Is Powerful

You, LORD, are our Father…
we are all the work of your hand.
– Isaiah 64:8

Mrs. Hall's Sunday-School Class

Mrs. Hall's Sunday-school class was learning about how Jesus taught His disciples to pray.

"Jesus said, 'Our Father in heaven,'" said Mrs. Hall.

Katie listened carefully. She had never met her own dad. Could she call God her Father like Jesus did? She raised her hand. "Does that mean Jesus shares His Father with us? I mean, why didn't Jesus pray 'My Father' instead of 'Our Father'?"

"Good question!" said Mrs. Hall. "We have earthly families, don't we? And they're all different."

Katie looked around the table at her classmates. *Charlie lived with his aunt. Jack had a stepmother. Andy was Lucy's cousin, but each of them had their own families. Mrs. Hall was right.*

"Each of us is also a member of God's family," Mrs. Hall went on. "We share the same heavenly Father as Jesus."

Charlie looked surprised. "Does that mean Jesus is actually our brother?" he asked.

Mrs. Hall smiled. "Yes. God is the Father of us all. That means Jesus is our brother. So when you pray the LORD's Prayer, you can say, 'Our Father' right along with Jesus."

Your Turn

1. What you think about Jesus being your brother?
2. Why are you considered part of God's family?

_____

_____

Prayer

My Father in heaven, I am glad that I am part of Your family and that Jesus is my brother. Amen.

God Is Powerful

You, LORD, are our Father...
we are all the work of your hand.
– Isaiah 64:80

You Can't Fool God

You can't fool God by praying what you think He wants to hear. What kind of prayer do you think God wants to hear from you? Cross out all the "X's" and write the remaining letters on the spaces to find out the honest way to pray.

X F X R X O X M   X T X H X E

_ _ _ _   _ _ _

X H X E A X R X T

_ _ _ _ _

Prayer

LORD, I can't fool You, and I don't want to. You know my heart. Help me be myself when I talk with You. Amen.

283

God Is Powerful

You, LORD, are our Father...
we are all the work of your hand.
– Isaiah 64:80

My God Shield

Do you remember God's armor? Connect the dots to see one way God protects you. Then look up and write out Ephesians 6:16 to see how this piece of armor protects you.

_____

_____

Prayer

Dear LORD, You are my Protector and my Shield. Remind me to pay attention when You warn me about danger. Amen.

God Is Powerful

You, LORD, are our Father…
we are all the work of your hand.
– Isaiah 64:80

God Knows

Victoria's brother was very sick. He was in the hospital, and the doctors didn't know if he would get better or not.

Victoria told her friend Alexis about her brother.

"I know how you feel," said Alexis. "My sister had her appendix burst. She had to have an operation. But she got better."

Victoria turned away. *Alexis doesn't understand exactly how I feel,* Victoria thought. *I feel alone and afraid. My brother might die.*

Alexis saw that Victoria was disappointed. "Victoria, I can't understand exactly how you feel. My sister's situation was different than your brother's." She paused. "I'm sorry your brother is sick. It's hard."

Alexis couldn't understand Victoria's situation exactly. People can know a little bit about how you feel, and they can show they care. But you are different than anyone else. Your thoughts and feelings are one of a kind.

God knows you. He understands your feelings. He knows your thoughts and your heart. You are never alone when you know your heavenly Father and His love for You.

Your Turn

1. Describe a time you told people how you felt and they didn't understand.
2. What helps you remember to talk to God when you feel alone?

_____

_____

_____

Prayer

God, I'm Your girl. I'm so glad You know me. Help me tell You how I feel and what I think. Amen.

God Is Powerful

*You, L*ORD*, are our Father...*
we are all the work of your hand.
– Isaiah 64:80

Your One-of-a-Kind Thoughts

Write down some one-of-a-kind thoughts and feelings you have that you think only God will understand. Talk to God about them.

Prayer

God, You are my heavenly Father, and I can talk to You about anything. I want to tell You everything about me, good and bad, because You love me no matter what. Amen.

God Is Powerful

You, LORD, are our Father…
we are all the work of your hand.
– Isaiah 64:80

God Is Your "Abba"

"Abba" is another name for God. Abba means "Daddy." You can call God Abba because He is your heavenly Daddy.

Color the poster to remind you that God is your heavenly Daddy who loves you perfectly.

Prayer

Abba, thank You for being my heavenly Daddy. Let me stay close to You. Amen.

God Is Powerful

You, LORD, are our Father...
we are all the work of your hand.
– Isaiah 64:80

#1 Dad

Your earthly dad is special, but your heavenly Father is the best of any dad...and anyone else. Color the ribbon to show you know your heavenly Father is the best.

Prayer

Heavenly Father, You are the best! Amen.

288

Jesus Is Alive!

[Jesus] was taken up before their very eyes,
and a cloud hid him from their sight.
– Acts 1:9

An Eyewitness Report

An "eyewitness" is a person who sees something happen. When you notice a bully stick out his foot so that another student trips and falls, you are an eyewitness. Your teacher may ask you to explain what you saw. What you tell her becomes an "eyewitness report."

Jesus' friends were eyewitnesses too. They saw Jesus alive after He had died on the cross. That is awesome! Some people have a hard time believing Jesus is real. He is! God wanted people to know, so He had Jesus' friends write their eyewitness reports.

In their reports, Jesus' friends explained what they saw after Jesus died. They told how and where Jesus went to see them. He talked with them and offered to let them touch Him so they would know He was real. He ate with them to show He was alive and well. Forty days after Jesus rose, His disciples witnessed Him rising to heaven in a cloud.

Jesus wanted His friends to be eyewitnesses to people that He lived, died, and rose from the dead. You can read an eyewitness account in John 20–21.

Your Turn

1. Why might it be hard for some people to believe Jesus is real?
2. How does having an eyewitness report help you know Jesus is alive?

_____

_____

_____

_____

Prayer

God, thank You for giving me an eyewitness report that Jesus is alive. I believe in Him. Amen.

Jesus Is Alive!

*[Jesus] was taken up before their very eyes,
and a cloud hid him from their sight.*
– Acts 1:9

Your Eyewitness Report

Write or draw your eyewitness report of what you know about God. Tell at least one thing you have seen God do.

Prayer

God, I am so glad You died for me so I can live with You in heaven for eternity. Amen.

Jesus Is Alive!

*[Jesus] was taken up before their very eyes,
and a cloud hid him from their sight.*
– Acts 1:9

The Holy Spirit

Do you have a favorite sweater or toy that makes you feel good? It comforts you. When Jesus went back to heaven, He promised his friends to ask God to send someone to comfort and guide them (John 14:16-17). God sent His Holy Spirit, who lives in your heart.

How long does the Holy Spirit live? Solve the puzzle to find out. Put an X through the first letter. Circle the second letter. Repeat this pattern for all the letters. When you're done, write the circled letters on the lines.

E F G O K R B E C V H E U R J

_____ _____ _____ _____ _____ _____!

Prayer

Lord Jesus, thank You for sending the Holy Spirit to live in me. Amen.

Jesus Is Alive!

[Jesus] was taken up before their very eyes,
and a cloud hid him from their sight.
– Acts 1:9

The Family Signal

Brooke's father got a job in a different city. He had to start work right away, but the family couldn't move into their new house for three weeks. Brooke's father had an idea. "I will move, start my job, and stay in a hotel until our house is ready. You keep living here until our new house is ready. I'll come back and get you."

"I think we can make that work," said Brooke's mom.

"We will have a special family signal so you know when it's time to move," said Brooke's father. "You will know when I call up and say, 'It's time to load the boxes!'"

Brooke spoke with her father every day. A week went by. Then one day, the telephone rang. Brooked answered.

"It's time to load the boxes!" said Brooke's father. That afternoon, his car pulled into the driveway. Brooke's father had kept his promise.

Jesus is the same way. He keeps His promises. He wants to talk with you every day so He can be close to you and you can be close to Him.

Your Turn

1. How does it feel when you are away from the people you love?
2. Have you thought about how great it will be to live with Jesus forever?

_____

_____

_____

Prayer

LORD, thank You for keeping Your promises. I want to be with You now and forever. Amen.

Jesus Is Alive!

[Jesus] was taken up before their very eyes,
and a cloud hid him from their sight.
– Acts 1:9

With You Forever

Someone wants to be with you forever—Jesus! Can you find His name in the word search?

Prayer

Jesus, thank You for being my LORD and Savior. Amen.

Jesus Is Alive!

[Jesus] was taken up before their very eyes,
and a cloud hid him from their sight.
– Acts 1:9

Jesus Cares!

Jesus wants to hear from you. Fill out the prayer, and then talk to Jesus.

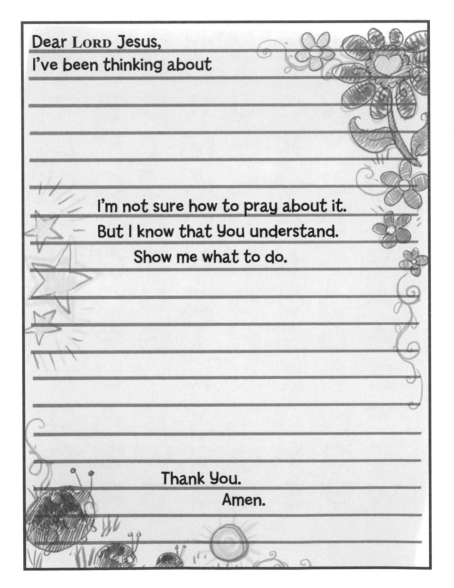

Dear LORD Jesus,
I've been thinking about

I'm not sure how to pray about it.
But I know that You understand.
Show me what to do.

Thank You.
Amen.

Jesus Is Alive!

[Jesus] was taken up before their very eyes,
and a cloud hid him from their sight.
– Acts 1:9

God's Family

You are a member of God's family. Add the names of your family and friends who are also part of God's family tree.

Prayer

Dear God, I am glad I am part of Your family. Amen.

295

The Book of Life

Rejoice that your names are written in heaven.
– Luke 10:20

Have You Signed Up?

Jayme and Connor stood in line to check in at basketball camp. The gym was crowded, but the twins were getting close to the front of the line.

"I heard the camp is full," said the kid standing behind the twins. "The leaders won't allow anyone in who didn't sign up ahead of time."

The girl standing in front of the boys reached the check-in table. "I don't understand," said the girl. "Why can't I attend camp?"

"Your name isn't on the list," said the coach. "Did you register ahead of time?"

The girl shook her head sadly.

"I'm sorry," said the coach. "Only those whose names are on this list can attend this session."

Jayme and Connor were next. They weren't worried. They had planned ahead and signed up early. Their names were on the list.

God has a "Book of Life" that lists the people who will live with Him forever. These people have chosen to believe in Jesus and accept His offer of forgiveness and eternal life. They follow Jesus.

Are you on Jesus' list? If not, talk to Jesus today. Ask Him into your heart as your LORD and Savior.

Your Turn

1. Why is it important you talk with Jesus about what you believe?
2. Have you told Jesus you believe in Him and know He died for you?

_____

_____

_____

Prayer

LORD, I believe in You. You are all-powerful yet chose to die for me and forgive my sin so I can be in Your family. I want to serve and worship You. Amen.

The Book of Life

Rejoice that your names are written in heaven.
– Luke 10:20

The Book of Life

If Jesus is your LORD and Savior and you choose to follow Him, your name is written in His Book of Life. As a reminder of that, write your name in this Book of Life. You can also write the names of people you know who believe in Jesus.

Prayer

LORD, I am so glad I believe You are my Savior and my name is written in Your Book of Life. I want to live with You forever. Amen.

The Book of Life

Rejoice that your names are written in heaven.
– Luke 10:20

God's Home

Do you know where the Book of Life is? It is with God. To find out where, follow the instructions. Color the shapes with "1" in purple. Color the shapes with "2" in yellow.

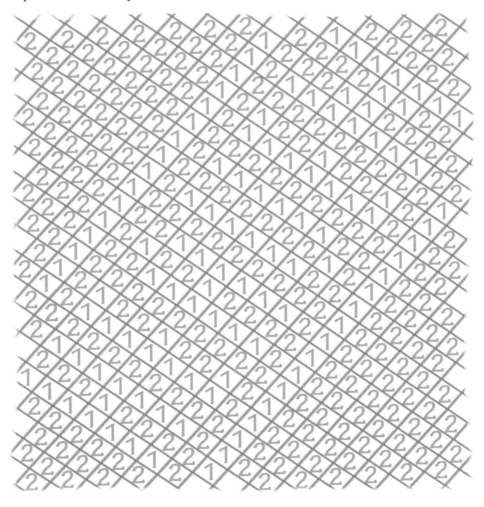

Prayer

Jesus, I am excited that someday I will meet You in person. Until then, thank You for being with me every day. Amen.

You Are in the Book of Life

Rejoice that your names are written in heaven.
– Luke 10:20

Heaven Is Real

There are things you do to get ready to go to a new place. You study a map. You look at photos. You talk with people who have been there. And you ask for directions.

Heaven is a real place, but getting there is different than going to the beach or taking a trip to the mountains. The Bible says people get to heaven in a special way. The apostle Paul wrote, "I tell you a mystery...we will all be changed" (1 Corinthians 15:51). That means you can't travel to heaven in a car or on an airplane. Instead, God decides when you are ready to go, and He takes care of everything. First, you will be changed. Then, in a twinkling of an eye, you will be with Him. But you have a lot God wants you to experience here on Earth first.

Jesus said, "The one who believes in me will live, even though they die; and whoever lives by believing in me will never die" (John 11:26-27). So grow in Jesus and live for and in Him. Someday you will go to heaven and be with Jesus forever.

Your Turn

1. How do you get to heaven?
2. What should you do until it is time for you to go to heaven?

_____

_____

_____

_____

Prayer

LORD Jesus, I believe in You. Help me walk with You and be close to You. I trust that when the time comes, You will guide me to heaven. Amen.

The Book of Life

Rejoice that your names are written in heaven.
– Luke 10:20

Trip to Heaven

Tell Jesus you believe in Him and want to live with Him in heaven someday. Using your pencil or crayon, help the girl get to Jesus.

Prayer

LORD, I believe You died for my sins and that I will live in heaven with You. Right now, help me study my Bible so I will understand how to live for You. Amen.

The Book of Life

Rejoice that your names are written in heaven.
– Luke 10:20

Your Room

Jesus said, "My Father's house has many rooms; if that were not so, would I have told you that I am going there to prepare a place for you?" (John 14:2). Draw a picture of yourself in this room while imagining the room Jesus is preparing for you in heaven.

Prayer

LORD, I am thankful You are thinking ahead and preparing a place for me with You in heaven. I love You. Amen.

The Book of Life

Rejoice that your names are written in heaven.
– Luke 10:20

Your Good Name

Proverbs 22:1 says, "A good name is more desirable than great riches." Have you talked to your parents about your name? Fill out this suitcase tag with your parents' help. Aren't you glad your name is in the Book of Life?

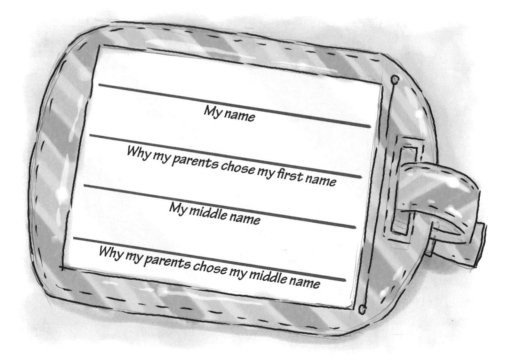

My name

Why my parents chose my first name

My middle name

Why my parents chose my middle name

Prayer

LORD God, thank You for loving me and wanting me to be with You here on Earth and in heaven. Amen.

God Is Your Rock

The name of the LORD is a fortified tower;
the righteous run to it and are safe.
– Proverbs 18:10

The Tree House

"I am not sure you should try climbing up the tree house ladder right now," Chad said. "Dad and I still need to pour concrete around the posts."

"Aw, come on," said Anna. "It looks good to me." Anna grabbed both sides of the ladder. She looked up at the tree house and took one step up, and then two. On the third step, Anna felt the ladder wobble. She jumped down to the ground.

Chad pointed to the holes around the ladder's legs and the tree-house posts. "The posts need to be secure to keep us safe," he said. "Come back on Wednesday to try again."

Anna nodded. Two days later, she stood in Chad's backyard. Chad showed her where his dad had poured concrete around the posts. Anna walked around the tree house. She put her arms around every post and tried to shake it. They were secure. Even the ladder felt strong and steady. She and Chad climbed up into the tree house.

Concrete helped make Chad's tree house secure. It was strong and couldn't be moved. God is like that. Psalm 18:2 says, "The LORD is my rock, my fortress and my deliverer; my God is my rock."

Your Turn

1. Name a time when things around you changed and it was hard.
2. How will it help you know God is your Rock when you have a bad day?

_____

_____

_____

Prayer

LORD, I am glad You are strong and secure. You can't be shaken. You are my Rock. Amen.

God Is Your Rock

The name of the LORD is a fortified tower;
the righteous run to it and are safe.
– Proverbs 18:10

Your Rock

Create a special reminder that you can count on God.

What You Need

- a small rock or stone
- smock or oversized shirt
- paint brush
- newspapers
- acrylic paints
- markers

What to Do

Wash your rock or stone. Let it dry thoroughly.

Spread newspapers on your work area. Use acrylic paints to paint your rock. Allow paint to dry completely. With markers, write "God is my Rock" on the painted rock and then decorate.

Keep your rock in a special place to remind you that you can always count on God.

Prayer

God, thank You for being my Rock I can depend on. Amen.

God Is Your Rock

The name of the LORD is a fortified tower;
the righteous run to it and are safe.
– Proverbs 18:10

Jesus Living in You

Do you have an aquarium? Maybe there is one at school. The fish have to be taken care of. The water has to be the right temperature, food needs to be good, and sometimes they need medicine. Jesus lives inside of you. He wants you to be strong in your faith by reading the Bible, praying, and growing closer to Him.

On each fish, write a way you can grow a strong faith when Jesus lives in you.

Prayer

LORD Jesus, thank You for paying the price for my sins so I can be close to You. You are my Rock and my Savior. I will be forever grateful. Amen.

God Is Your Rock

The name of the LORD is a fortified tower;
the righteous run to it and are safe.
– Proverbs 18:10

A Name that Fits

Dan was named after his father, Danny, and his grandfather Daniel.

Michaela's parents have a close friend, Michael, who helped them during a hard time in their lives. To honor him, they named their daughter after him.

Noelle's parents hadn't picked a name for her. When she was born close to Christmas, they chose "Noelle"—the French word for "Christmas."

Your parents chose your name. Maybe you were named for a family member or to honor a special person. Maybe your parents simply liked how your name sounded.

Things were different in Bible times. Most names had specific meanings. People understood that a name was really a piece of information about a person. God has many names, each one showing something about who He is. For instance, "Almighty God" means God is all-powerful. "Savior" means God is the One who saves you from sin.

God has lots of wonderful traits. The Bible says, "The name of the LORD is a fortified tower" (Proverbs 18:10). In other words, "God is strong and provides protection." You can study God's names to learn what He is like. God's names show He is someone you can count on.

Your Turn

1. What do you know about your name?
2. Why is it helpful to learn about God's names?

_____

_____

_____

Prayer

LORD God, I want to know Your names and what they mean. Amen.

306

God Is Your Rock

The name of the LORD is a fortified tower;
the righteous run to it and are safe.
– Proverbs 18:10

Every Knee Should Bow

When you talk to God and about God, you use God's names or refer to Him respectfully as Father, Daddy, God Almighty. Another way to show respect is to bow. Philippians 2:10 says, "At the name of Jesus every knee should bow." People bow by getting on their knees, bending at the waist, or just lowering their heads. Circle the people who must not know Jesus yet.

Prayer

LORD, help me always treat You and Your names with respect and love. Amen.

God Is Your Rock

The name of the LORD is a fortified tower;
the righteous run to it and are safe.
– Proverbs 18:10

Are You Perfect?

Do you think you can be good if you try hard? Can you be perfect if you are careful? The truth is, you can't. Only God can be perfect. Only God can be good all the time. How can you be the best you can be? Replace each number with a letter from the key to find the answer.

I'm not perfect but the

___ ___ ___ ___   ___ ___ ___
1   6   3   2   6   8   4

can change me!

8 = N   1 = H
6 = O   3 = L
2 = Y   4 = E

Prayer

LORD, You are the Holy One. Help me become more like You every day. Amen.

God Is Your Rock

The name of the LORD is a fortified tower;
the righteous run to it and are safe.
– Proverbs 18:10

Find the Lost Sheep

You can count on God to protect you and watch over you. God is your good Shepherd. He won't let you get lost or wander away if you talk to Him. Find and circle the five sheep at this farm.

Prayer

LORD, You are my Shepherd. Thank You for knowing me, caring for me, watching over me, and protecting me. Amen.

God Is Your Light

[Jesus] said, "I am the light of the world. Whoever follows me will never walk in darkness, but will have the light of life."

–John 8:12

Lost!

Marissa woke up in her tent at camp. She had to use the bathroom. "Chloe, are you awake?"

Chloe groaned. "Yes…"

Marissa grabbed her flashlight. The girls crept outside and walked down the path. They heard talking and laughter. "It sounds like there are people down there," said Chloe. "The bathroom must be that way." The girls turned to the right.

There were shadows along the path, and nothing looked familiar. "This doesn't seem right." Marissa said. She flicked on the flashlight.

"I guess we took a wrong turn," said Chloe. "I'm glad you've got a flashlight."

Marissa and Chloe learned how easy it is to get lost. They followed people's voices and assumed it was the right way. When they finally turned on the flashlight, they were able to get back on track.

God is your Light. He helps you make good choices. When you read the Bible, pray, and listen to the Holy Spirit. It is like turning on a flashlight from God. He will help you stay on the right path.

Your Turn

1. Why did the girls get lost?
2. How can God, your Light, help you each day?

Prayer

LORD, You are my Light. Amen.

God Is Your Light

[Jesus] said, "I am the light of the world. Whoever follows me will never walk in darkness, but will have the light of life."
–John 8:12

Don't Block the Light

What happens when light is blocked? How can you keep God's Light on in your life? Here's an interesting activity you'll enjoy.

What You Need
- a darkened room ■ a flashlight
- small objects
- a partner (perhaps a parent)

What to Do

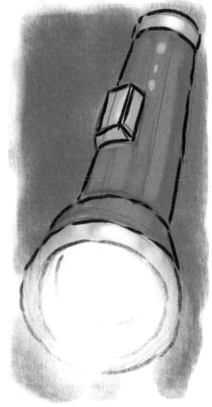

Ask your parents for permission to help you do this activity.

- Gather materials and go into a darkened room.
- Turn on the flashlight. Shine it onto a wall, door, or other surface.
- Have your partner hold up one of the objects in front of the flashlight beam. What happens to the light on the wall?
- Have your partner lower the object so that the flashlight beam is not blocked. What happens to the light in the room?
- Repeat these steps using the other objects.

God is Light. What gets in the way of His Light shining in your life? How can you keep His Light at full power?

Prayer

LORD, shine Your light in my entire life. I want to shine for You. Amen.

311

God Is Your Light

[Jesus] said, "I am the light of the world. Whoever follows
me will never walk in darkness, but will have the light of life."
–John 8:12

Always with Us

One of God's names is "Immanuel." It means "God with us." Jesus came
to Earth and lived for a while. Now He's back in heaven. Is He still your
Immanuel when He's not here physically? Find out by substituting each
number with the letter from the key.

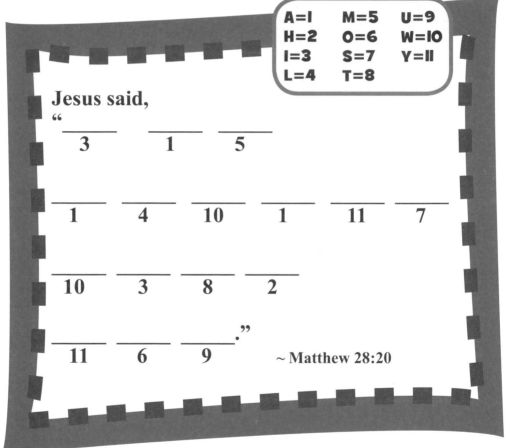

A=1   M=5   U=9
H=2   O=6   W=10
I=3   S=7   Y=11
L=4   T=8

Jesus said,
"
___ ___ ___
3   1   5

___ ___ ___ ___ ___ ___
1 4 10 1 11 7

___ ___ ___ ___
10 3 8 2

___ ___ ___."
11 6 9   ~ Matthew 28:20

Prayer

God, thank You for being with me always. Thank You for sending Jesus,
my Immanuel, so I can know You better. Amen.

God Is Your Light

[Jesus] said, "I am the light of the world. Whoever follows me will never walk in darkness, but will have the light of life."

–John 8:12

You Can't See the Wind

"Look at the wind!" shouted Katie who was standing at the front window. Trees swayed and leaves blew in circles. The flag hanging on the front porch whipped around its pole twice. *Whoosh! Whee!*

Katie's older brother, Joshua, walked over to the window. "You can't see the wind. It's invisible. Wind is air that's moving around."

Katie pointed to the shrubs. "But I can see our holly bushes moving back and forth. Isn't that the wind?"

Josh laughed. "You just answered your own question! You said, 'I see the holly bushes moving.' You see what the wind *does* to the holly bushes—not the wind itself."

God's Spirit is like the wind. You may hear it, but you can't see it. Katie and Joshua saw how the wind moved through their trees and bushes. You can do the same thing to see God's Spirit moving. Look carefully. The Holy Spirit comes to people in ways you may not expect. Ask God to help you see His Spirit working in people. Ask God to help you worship Him and let His Spirit work in your heart and life. Then you can bend His way.

Your Turn

1. Why did Katie think she could "see the wind"?
2. In what ways is God's Spirit like the wind?
3. How can you see God's Spirit at work?

_____

_____

_____

Prayer

God, I need Your help to see Your Spirit working. I want Your Spirit to work in me too. Amen.

God Is Your Light

[Jesus] said, "I am the light of the world. Whoever follows me will never walk in darkness, but will have the light of life."
–John 8:12

The Holy Spirit at Work

"The wind blows wherever it pleases. You hear its sound, but you cannot tell where it comes from or where it is going. So it is with everyone born of the Spirit" (John 3:8). Complete the prayer, and then pray it with your heart.

Dear God,

I can hear the wind (pause and listen for a breeze or a blowing sound). I don't know where it comes from or how it forms.

But I know that the wind is real because I see it blowing through:

(look out your window and name things blowing in the wind).

I know Your Spirit is real because I see You working in

(name people who show the love of God to you).

I don't know what the wind will do next. And I don't know what Your Spirit will do next. But I am listening and watching. (Pause and listen quietly for how God wants to show Himself to you.)

Show me and help me see You at work today.

Amen.

314

God Is Your Light

[Jesus] said, "I am the light of the world. Whoever follows me will never walk in darkness, but will have the light of life."
–John 8:12

The Joy of Learning

God gives you many opportunities and ways to learn about Him. Look at each picture and describe how each situation is an opportunity to grow spiritually.

Prayer

LORD, You are my Teacher and LORD. Please teach me Your ways so I will always walk in Your Light. Amen.

315

God Is Your Light

[Jesus] said, "I am the light of the world. Whoever follows me will never walk in darkness, but will have the light of life."

–John 8:12

God Keeps You Safe

When people fall into deep water and need help, rescuers throw them a ring buoy. This helps the person float. God gives us ways to help us "float" when we are close to trouble. Write inside each ring buoy something you need help with today. Then talk to Jesus about each one.

Prayer

Lord God, I know I need Your help to live the right way—Your way. I want to make good choices every day. Amen.

God Is Awesome

The LORD Most High is awesome,
the great King over all the earth.

– Psalm 47:2

The Mountain and the Ant

Brittany and her family were on vacation. They drove a long time, and eventually Brittany fell asleep.

"Wow!" When Brittany woke up, she saw that the view had changed. "Wow!" she exclaimed again. She saw large, purple mountains with pure white, snowy tops. "The mountains are awesome!" she said.

"Yes," said Dad. "And we're not even that close. You'll see how huge they really are when we get nearer."

Brittany felt a tickle. She looked down. A tiny ant crept down her arm. "It looks like we picked up a visitor when we stopped for our picnic," she said, studying the ant. "It's so little, and the mountains are so big."

"Now, that's awesome!" said her mom. "God made both of them."

God is the Creator. He thought up ideas of things that would be good to have on the Earth: different kinds of land, water, plants, colors, and weather.

Then, after thinking up those ideas, God made all of them. He did it all by Himself. He is amazing.

Your Turn

1. Do you think God had to work hard to think up what to put in the world?
2. What are some awesome things about our world?

Prayer

LORD, You are awesome! I praise You. Amen.

God Is Awesome

The LORD Most High is awesome, the great King over all the earth.
– Psalm 47:2

God Is Greater

Do you know the ">" symbol? It means "greater than" or "bigger than." For example, 2 > 1 means "two is greater than one."

Let's use the ">" symbol to tell how great God is. On each line, write something that God is greater than!

God > than

God is greater than people.

God > than

God is greater than the world

God > than

God is greater than pastors.

Prayer

LORD God, You are King of everything. I humble myself before You. You are great, and I need You. Please make Your home in my heart. Amen.

God Is Awesome

The LORD Most High is awesome, the great King over all the earth.
– Psalm 47:2

God's Awesome World

Draw pictures of some things God made for your awesome world.

Prayer

Heavenly Father, when I look at this beautiful world, I want to praise You. You thought of everything! Amen.

God Is Awesome

The LORD Most High is awesome, the great King over all the earth.

– Psalm 47:2

You Are Special to God

"I like being with Corrie," Alexa told her mom. "But not so much with Bethany."

If you're like Alexa, there are some people you enjoy. Corrie makes Alexa laugh, and they have fun together. They talk easily, and Alexa likes Corrie's sense of humor. They may not always agree about everything, but both girls listen to each other.

On the other hand, Alexa feels uncomfortable around Bethany. For some reason, she and Bethany just don't connect. Alexa could hang around with her, but it would feel awkward. Bethany is nice and they get along at school, but they don't click together. Alexa chooses not to spend much time with Bethany.

Think about this: *God likes you!* He wants to be around you all the time. He wants to talk with you and listen to you. He's not just getting along with you—He likes you exactly the way you are. In fact, the Bible says God enjoys you so much that He wants everyone to know you are His friend. The King of heaven takes delight in you!

Your Turn

1. Which of your friends is easy for you to like? Who is harder to understand?
2. If God enjoys being with you, what are some ways you can be with HIm?

_____

_____

_____

Prayer

LORD God, it feels so good to know You enjoy being with me. Amen.

God Is Awesome

The Lord Most High is awesome, the great King over all the earth.
– Psalm 47:2

A Crown from Your King

God loves you so much He wants everyone to know it. Psalm 149:4 says, "The Lord takes delight in his people; he crowns the humble with victory." Draw a crown on the girl, and color her so she looks like you.

Prayer

Lord Jesus, I am so thankful that You—the great King over all the universe—came to die for me. Thank You! Amen.

God Is Awesome

The LORD Most High is awesome, the great King over all the earth.
– Psalm 47:2

Showing Jesus' Love

Look at the pictures and describe a way someone in each situation has an opportunity to show Jesus' love.

Prayer

God, I want You to be alive in me. Help me show kindness to people today in Your name. Amen.

God Is Awesome

The Lord Most High is awesome, the great King over all the earth.
– Psalm 47:2

Praising Your King

Read these verses from Psalm 149. Circle the words that show different ways you can praise God, your King.

Let Israel rejoice in their Maker;

let the people of Zion be glad in their King.

Let them praise his name with dancing

and make music to him with timbrel and harp.

Psalm 149:2-3

Prayer

God, I am so happy You are my King. Anytime is a good time to praise You! Amen.

God's Ways Always Work

The plans of the LORD stand firm forever.
– Psalm 33:11

The Decision

Lauren followed Shelby and Sam around to the back of their house. It was hot, and she was glad her friends had invited her over to cool off in their backyard.

Lauren set down her towel away from the water sprinkler. "Where's the spigot?" she asked. "I'll turn on the water."

Something seemed different from before.

"What's going on?" asked Lauren.

Sam pulled out a pack of cigarettes. "C'mon," he said. "Let's hide under the porch. We can try these. I snatched them from my dad."

Lauren gasped and turned to Shelby. "I thought we were going to play water games," Lauren said.

Shelby shrugged. "Our plans changed. Are you in or out?"

Lauren picked up her towel. "I am out. I would rather stick to doing things the way I know they work."

"What do you mean?" asked Shelby.

"Like doing what's right and pleasing God," said Lauren.

Your Turn

1. Why does doing the right thing always work?
2. How can you know what God wants?
3. Have you ever had to say no to your friends?

_____

_____

_____

Prayer

God, teach me Your ways. Help me be ready to make good choices. I know Your ways always work. Amen.

God's Ways Always Work

The plans of the LORD stand firm forever.
– Psalm 33:11

Doing It God's Way

Jesus' ways are always the best and always work. Start at the bottom and find your way to Jesus without getting sidetracked in a bad decision.

Prayer

God, I know if I follow Your rules I can't go wrong because Your ways are perfect. Amen.

God's Ways Always Work

The plans of the LORD stand firm forever.
– Psalm 33:11

Your Thankful List

Make a list of hard things that happened to you today or last week. Give God thanks and ask Him to help you grow in Him.

Prayer

LORD God, show me how to grow from everything that happens in my life. I'm thankful that You care about me and want me to do things Your way. Amen.

God's Ways Always Work

The plans of the LORD stand firm forever.
– Psalm 33:11

God's Way Can Be Hard

Mackenzie didn't want to visit Aunt Doris. As Mackenzie's mother parked the car, Mackenzie groaned. "Why do I have to go in?" she asked.

"It's the right thing to do," said her mom. Together they climbed the stairs to the second floor. Aunt Doris' door was open.

"Welcome!" she said, hugging Mackenzie and her mom.

Suddenly Mackenzie saw a ball of fur at Aunt Doris' feet.

Her aunt scooped up a wriggling kitten. "Do you like Felix? He is just two months old."

Mackenzie ran a finger over Felix's fur. The kitten reached out and batted at her finger. Mackenzie laughed.

"I got him to keep me company," said Aunt Doris. "But I thought you'd enjoy playing with him too."

Although Mackenzie dragged her feet, she did the right thing. Mackenzie enjoyed the visit, Aunt Doris was happy because she liked being with Mackenzie, and God was pleased.

Your Turn

1. Name a time when you didn't feel like doing something but did it anyway because it was the right thing to do.
2. Why does God want you to do the right things?
3. How will God help you follow His will?

_____

_____

_____

Prayer

LORD God, Your ways are always good. Sometimes I don't want to do them, but help me do Your will always. Amen.

God's Ways Always Work

The plans of the LORD stand firm forever.
– Psalm 33:11

The Right Way

How can you know what the right thing to do is? Pray! Solve the puzzle to discover what you should do first. Substitute each symbol for the letter in the key.

+	$	!	@	%	

*	$	+	(

#	(

?	(	<	)

>	^	&	&

~ Psalm 143:10

Key:

A = !
C = @
D = #
E = $
H = %
I = ^
L = &
M = *
O = (
R =)
T = +
U = <
W = >
Y = ?

Prayer

LORD, please teach me to do Your will. I know the plans You have for me are good, so help me make the right choices. Amen.

328

God's Ways Always Work

The plans of the LORD stand firm forever.
– Psalm 33:11

Plans Puzzle

Can you find and circle the four words that describe God's desire for you?

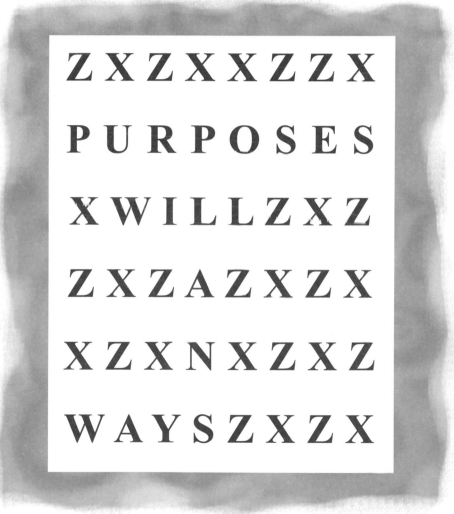

Prayer

God, I know Your ways are best. I might not understand Your will, so show me in the Bible what I need to know. Amen.

God's Ways Always Work

The plans of the LORD stand firm forever.
– Psalm 33:11

The Path to God's Kingdom

Help these friends find God's kingdom. Trace the most direct route.

Prayer

LORD, I pray that Your kingdom will grow. Show me people You want me to share Your love with. Amen.

Working with God

We are God's handiwork,
created in Christ Jesus to do good works.

– Ephesians 2:10

The Copycat

Lily's brother, John, was two years old and liked to do the same things Lily did.

"He's a copycat," she complained, throwing down her book.

John picked up the book and threw it down. He smiled.

"That's just how he learns," explained Mom. "He watches what you do, and then he does the same thing."

Lily thought for a minute. "Are you sure he's not doing it just to make me mad?"

"I am sure," said Mom. "But why don't you see for yourself? Do something kind, and see if he does it too."

"Okay," said Lily. She walked over to her mom and hugged her. "I love you, Mom."

John watched. He toddled over to Mom and grabbed her legs. "Wuv you!" he said.

Lily and Mom laughed. Mom hugged Lily and hugged John. "I love you too," she said.

People are watching how you treat others. When you are a Christian, you show God's love by how you act toward them.

Your Turn

1. Who was watching Lily? Who is watching you?
2. What are three ways you can show God's love in your actions?

_____

_____

_____

Prayer

LORD, help me show Your love in the things I do. Amen.

Working with God

We are God's handiwork, created in Christ Jesus to do good works.
– Ephesians 2:10

Helping God

How does God want you to help Him? By being kind and loving people in His name. Draw a picture of a way you can help someone this week.

Prayer

Dear God, show me how to be more helpful according to Your will. Amen.

Working with God

We are God's handiwork, created in Christ Jesus to do good works.
– Ephesians 2:10

Reflecting God's Love

Jesus said, "Let the little children come to me." He loved children. Draw a picture on the mirror of how you can reflect Jesus' love to girls and boys you meet.

Prayer

God, You want me to do good things in Your name. Help me honor You in what I say and do. Amen.

God's Awesome Word

We are God's handiwork,
created in Christ Jesus to do good works.

– Ephesians 2:10

Holly's Fresh Start

Mom came into the room and sat down next to Holly.

"I am so sorry, Mom," said Holly. "I feel awful," said Holly. "I don't think you'll ever love me again."

"Holly, I will always love you, no matter what." Mom stood up and walked to Holly's calendar. She pointed to the date. "Give me a pen, Holly," she said. She took the black marker Holly handed her and made a large "X" through that day's box. "You made a mistake today, Holly, but you are sorry for it."

Holly nodded.

Mom pointed to the box on the calendar for the next day. "Tomorrow is a new day. You get to start over again."

Holly looked at today's box. It was crossed out, but the box for the next day was clean. "That sounds good," she said. "I can have a fresh start."

God doesn't want you to carry around your mistakes. When you tell God you are sorry, He forgives you. Just like Holly, you get a fresh start.

Your Turn

1. Why is it important to tell God you are sorry for your mistakes?
2. How do you get a fresh start?

_____

_____

Prayer

Jesus, I am sorry when I don't follow You and Your ways. Thank You for forgiving me. I want to be clean and new in You. Amen.

Working with God

We are God's handiwork, created in Christ Jesus to do good works.

– Ephesians 2:10

Crossing Out Mistakes

In the left boxes, write mistakes people (including you) make. Now cross them out with an "X." In the boxes on the right, draw pictures of clean hearts to remind you that Jesus forgives you when you ask.

Prayer

Heavenly Father, everyone makes mistakes, including me. When I do, please remind me to quickly say I am sorry and ask You to forgive me. Amen.

Working with God

We are God's handiwork, created in Christ Jesus to do good works.
– Ephesians 2:10

Home of Righteousness

Revelation 21:12 and 21 say that heaven has a holy city with twelve gates decorated with jewels. Color and decorate one of the heavenly gates.

Prayer

Father, I pray I will do things Your way here on earth, just like those good ways are always done in heaven. Amen.

Working with God

We are God's handiwork, created in Christ Jesus to do good works.

– Ephesians 2:10

With Jesus Forever

Victoria was sad because her grandmother had died. Grandma always let Victoria dress up in her old, fancy clothes and special hats. Victoria's mom told her that someday she would see her grandmother again…in heaven. On each hat, write the name of a person you want to know and be with forever. Pray for each person. Ask God to help them know and believe in Jesus. Amen.

Prayer

Lord Jesus, I need You. I believe in You. I want to be with You forever. I want those I love to be with You forever too. Amen.

God Meets Your Needs

God will meet all your needs according to the riches of his glory in Christ Jesus.

– Philippians 4:19

Jackie's Sneakers

Jackie and her mother were shopping for school clothes. Jackie saw a pair of blue-and-white sneakers. "These are perfect!" she said. "Please, Mom, may I have them?"

Mom studied the list they had made together the night before. "I don't see 'sneakers' here," she said. She looked at Jackie. "Think hard. Are new sneakers a 'need' or a 'want'?"

There is a big difference between what you need and what you want. Needs are what you must have to live and grow in healthy ways. Wants are what you'd like to have but can live without. It can be easy to get the two mixed up. One way to check if it is a want or need is to ask this question: "Is this something I need today to live God's way?"

God knows what you need. He promises to give it to you if you ask. He will meet your needs every day.

Your Turn

1. Why is it easy to get "needs" and "wants" mixed up?
2. Name a time when you wanted something that wasn't a need. What was it?
3. How does God meet your needs? (Hint: Read today's Bible verse.)

_____

_____

_____

_____

Prayer

God, help me learn the difference between needs and wants. Amen.

God Meets Your Needs

God will meet all your needs according to the riches of his glory in Christ Jesus.

– Philippians 4:19

Is It a Need or a Want?

Look at this list. If it is a need for a healthy life, put an "N" in the box. If it is a want, put a "W" in the box.

☐ a safe place to live

☐ being first in line

☐ eating a healthy lunch

☐ knowing Jesus

☐ new nail polish

☐ people I can love

☐ popularity

☐ the best spelling grade in the class

☐ the chance to learn

☐ warm clothes

☐ watching my favorite TV show today

☐ winning a game

Prayer

LORD, sometimes I mistake a need for a want, and then I get upset when I don't get it. Please work in my heart so I will be content with what You provide. Amen.

God Meets Your Needs

*God will meet all your needs according to the
riches of his glory in Christ Jesus.*

– Philippians 4:19

The Bread of Life

Jesus said, "I am the bread of life." What did He mean? To find out, put
these words in the right order. If you need help, read John 6:33 NLT.

**TO   ONE   THE   AND   FROM   LIFE   DOWN   WORLD
WHO   GIVES   COMES   HEAVEN   THE**

____ ____ ____ ____   ____ ____ ____

____ ____ ____ ____   ____ ____ ____

____ ____ ____ ____   ____ ____ ____ ____

____ ____ ____   ____ ____ ____ ____

____ ____ ____   ___ ___

____ ___ ____   ____ ____ ____ ____ ____.   ~ John 6:33

Prayer

Lᴏʀᴅ, You are my Bread of Life. Help me do my part in getting fed
physically and spiritually by bringing my needs to You. Amen.

God Meets Your Needs

God will meet all your needs according to the riches of his glory in Christ Jesus.

– Philippians 4:19

Talia Takes a Break

"Water break!" called Coach Lou.

Megan walked to the sideline. She grabbed her water bottle and took a long drink. Then she joined her teammates under a tree. The air was still. Even in the shade, Megan felt drops of sweat trickling down her back. The break felt good. Megan knew she needed rest in order to finish the second half of soccer practice.

Megan noticed one team member still walking in. "It looks like Talia doesn't feel well." She watched as Talia stopped and put her hands over her eyes. She bent down on one knee. Megan jumped up and ran to Talia.

Coach Lou joined her. "Let's get you out of the sun, Talia."

In the shade, Megan pressed a cool cloth to Talia's forehead. Coach Lou gave her a cup of water.

"Drink this and give your body a break," Coach said. "Sit here and watch the rest of practice. I need you rested for our game on Saturday."

Talia needed rest and water. Your body needs rest too. God wants you to be healthy, so make sure you take breaks when you need to, drink water, and get plenty of sleep at night.

Your Turn

1. When is it hard to remember to take a break?
2. Why does God want you to get enough rest?

_____

_____

_____

Prayer

God, You provide chances for me to get rest. Help me do my part by taking breaks, drinking water, and getting enough sleep. Amen.

God Meets Your Needs

*God will meet all your needs according to the
riches of his glory in Christ Jesus.*

– Philippians 4:19

Types of Rest

Think about times you need rest. Color each girl. Write a thank-You
prayer to God for rest beside each one.

Prayer

God, please help me slow down when I need rest. Amen.

God Meets Your Needs

*God will meet all your needs according to the
riches of his glory in Christ Jesus.*

– Philippians 4:19

What God's Strength Looks Like

God uses "word pictures" in the Bible to help you understand how He works. A word picture is an example you can see in your mind. In Isaiah 40:31, God uses word pictures to describe what happens to people when He gives them strength. Look at the picture and think of a way God has given you strength.

Those who hope in the LORD will renew their strength.

They will soar on wings like eagles;

they will run and not grow weary,

they will walk and not be faint.

Prayer

God, I need You throughout the day. I put my hope in You for renewed strength. Amen.

God Meets Your Needs

God will meet all your needs according to the riches of his glory in Christ Jesus.

– Philippians 4:19

Choices You Make

Look at the pictures. Think of two choices for each one—one that pleases God and one that won't. Write down the one that pleases God.

Prayer

LORD, thank You for giving me choices. I'm glad You will help me stop and think so I can make choices that will please You. Amen.

God Gives You Relationships

This is the day the LORD has made.
We will rejoice and be glad in it.

– Psalm 118:24 NLT

Feeling Alone

Julia felt sad. Her best friend, Avery, had moved away on Saturday. Now it was Monday morning, and Julia felt alone. She dragged her feet along the sidewalk to school. She came to the crosswalk.

"Good morning, Julia!" said Mrs. Blackwell, the crossing guard. "How is my Sunshine Girl today?"

Julia smiled. She didn't feel so alone. She got to her classroom a few minutes early. A new girl with braids sat in one of the desks.

"Julia, I'm glad you are here," said her teacher. "This is Sonia's first day. Will you show her around the school?"

Julia nodded eagerly. She didn't feel so alone.

Later, on the way to recess, Julia walked past the basketball court.

"Hey, Julia!" shouted Tom. "We need another player. Come on."

Julia ran onto the court, and Tom tossed her the ball. She didn't feel so alone.

No one can take the place of a close friend, but God puts people in your path you can be friends with. Do what Julia did: Be a friend back.

Your Turn

1. Julia learned she had different kinds of friends. Describe them.
2. What did Julia do to not feel so alone.

_____

_____

_____

Prayer

God, thank You for putting different friends in my life. Amen.

345

God Gives You Relationships

*This is the day the L*ORD *has made.*
We will rejoice and be glad in it.

– Psalm 118:24 NLT

My Friends

Julia discovered that she has different kinds of friends. So do you. Your friends can be girls and boys your age, older children, and grown-ups. Look at the pictures and think of a friend you have that fits each picture. Pray for each friend you name and thank God for them!

Prayer

Dear God, when I think about it, I realize I have lots of friends. Thank You. Amen.

God Gives You Relationships

This is the day the LORD has made.
We will rejoice and be glad in it.

– Psalm 118:24 NLT

Hurts in Your Heart

People are never perfect. Even your best friend can hurt your feelings. With God's love, you can still be friends. Ask God to heal your heart when it hurts. His love will make you whole again.

God loves you no matter what. Read each example. Name a heart hurt that goes with it, and write your answers in the heart. If you experience any of them, ask God to heal your heart.

How I feel when a friend
says something unkind.

How I feel when I disobey.

How I feel when I do poorly at an activity.

How I feel when I'm not included.

How I feel when
I don't understand.

Prayer

LORD, You are the mighty Healer. When You see that my heart has been hurt, please heal me and help me forgive the person who hurt me. Amen.

347

God Gives You Relationships

*This is the day the LORD has made.
We will rejoice and be glad in it.*

– Psalm 118:24 NLT

A Change in Attitude

DeSandra just couldn't understand it. Yesterday had been so perfect. She and her brother, Jayden, went swimming. Then they'd had ice cream and played together all day. She was happy all day.

But today DeSandra was not happy. Mom asked her to help hang the sheets on a clothesline. Then they picked green beans in the garden. It was sunny and pretty outside, but it was also very hot. DeSandra sweated. Mosquitoes bit her. Even when Mom told her to take a break and drink some lemonade, DeSandra felt grumpy.

DeSandra forgot one important thing: her attitude. She'd had fun yesterday with Jayden as they played, but she could have also had a good time with her mom taking care of household chores and the garden. She could have enjoyed being with her mom and talking.

Each morning when you wake up, you get a special present from God: a new day. You make the choice to be glad about your day or to be mad about your day. How you use each new day is your gift to God.

Your Turn

1. What could DeSandra have done differently on the second day?
2. How does attitude make a difference in your day?
3. Why does God allow you to choose your attitude?

_____

_____

_____

Prayer

LORD, today You have given me a new day. I will rejoice and be glad in it! Amen.

God Gives You Relationships

This is the day the LORD has made.
We will rejoice and be glad in it.

– Psalm 118:24 NLT

A New Week

Color the picture of the calendar, and remember that every day is a new day!

Sunday	Monday	Tuesday	Wednesday	Thursday	Friday	Saturday

Prayer

LORD, I know You have given me the gifts of a new day and more opportunities to do what is right. Thank You. Amen.

God Gives You Relationships

This is the day the Lord has made.
We will rejoice and be glad in it.

– Psalm 118:24 NLT

You Can Be Strong!

When do you feel scared or nervous?The Bible says, "Do not be terrified" because God is with you. Draw a picture of a situation when you might feel scared. What will help you be brave? Who might God send to help or encourage you?

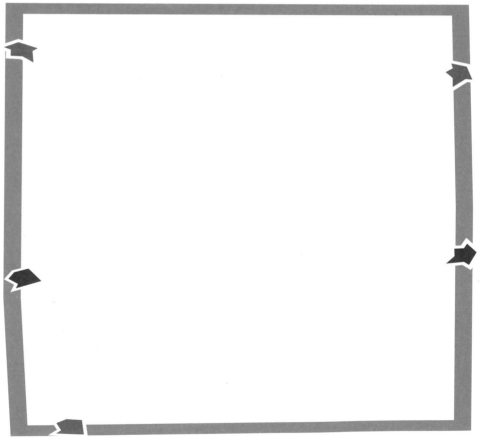

Prayer

Lord God, I want to cheerfully serve You even when I am nervous. Please give me Your strength and someone to encourage me. Amen.

God Gives You Relationships

*This is the day the L*ORD *has made.*
We will rejoice and be glad in it.

– Psalm 118:24 NLT

Special Gifts from God

A "gift" can be a talent others can see. It can also be a trait that's part of your personality. What kinds of gifts do you see in these pictures? Do you know people who have these gifts?

Prayer

God, You created me with special gifts. Help me learn what they are. Show me how to use my special gifts for You and to encourage others. Amen.

Confessing and Forgiving

If we confess our sins, he is faithful and just and will forgive us our sins and purify us from all unrighteousness.

– 1 John 1:9

God Sees Everything

Baby Gabrielle screamed, and Mama came running. "What happened to the baby?" she asked.

"I don't know," said Maria.

Mama picked up Gabrielle. There was a red mark on the baby's arm. "Maria, do you know anything about this?"

Maria shook her head, but she was lying. She had gotten mad at Gabrielle when the baby had grabbed her hair. Maria had slapped the baby's arm.

Mama soothed the baby and then put her in her crib.

Maria was afraid of being punished for hitting her baby sister. She didn't want Mama to know about it. But Maria was feeling sad and guilty. She knew she had done two things wrong: slap her sister and lie to her mama. She couldn't get it out of her mind.

Mama didn't see Maria hit Gabrielle, but God did. He sees everything.

God promises to forgive you for your mistakes. However, you must first tell Him what you did and say you are sorry. When you ask Him for forgiveness, He will forgive you. God will take away that bad feeling inside.

Your Turn

1. What must you do for God to forgive your mistakes?
2. Why do you think God wants you to confess your mistakes?
3. How does confessing your mistakes to God make you feel afterward?

_____

_____

_____

Prayer

LORD, I confess I have made mistakes. I am glad You are always ready to listen and forgive. Amen.

Confessing and Forgiving

*If we confess our sins, he is faithful and just and will
forgive us our sins and purify us from all unrighteousness.*

– 1 John 1:9

God Sees Your Mistakes

God sees all your mistakes, even the ones you hope are secret and hidden.
In this picture, there are eight "X's." Each "X" represents a mistake—and
God sees each one. Find and circle the "X's."

Prayer

God, thank You for forgiving me when I do or say something wrong and
confess it to You. Please make me brave and help me make things right
with people I hurt when I did wrong. Amen.

Confessing and Forgiving

If we confess our sins, he is faithful and just and will forgive us our sins and purify us from all unrighteousness.

– 1 John 1:9

The Right Direction

Will you help the girl reach the cross? You may have to turn around and go in a different direction sometimes.

Prayer

LORD, help me recognize when I am about to do something wrong. Give me the courage to turn away and follow Your path. Amen.

Confessing and Forgiving

If we confess our sins, he is faithful and just and will forgive us our sins and purify us from all unrighteousness.

– 1 John 1:9

Ming's Debt

"May I borrow a dollar to buy some chips and a drink?" Ming asked her friend Yan. They were at the refreshment stand in the park. Ming was hungry and thirsty. "I'll pay you back tomorrow at school."

"Sure," said Yan, handing Ming the money. "But please remember to pay me back tomorrow. I need that dollar to pay my library fee."

"I promise I'll remember," Ming said.

The next morning, Ming saw Yan waiting for her in front of their classroom.

"Did you remember to bring the money?" Yan asked.

Ming frowned. She had forgotten. Yan had been kind to her, and now Yan would get in trouble for not paying her library fee.

Ming owed Yan, so Ming was in debt to Yan for the borrowed money.

In the LORD's Prayer, you ask God to forgive your debts. That's a special way of asking God to forgive you for your mistakes. It's like saying, "LORD, I was wrong. I'm in debt to You. Please forgive me."

That's the kind of prayer God loves to hear. He will forgive your debt when you tell Him you're sorry for not obeying Him.

Your Turn

1. Why is asking God to forgive your "debts" like asking Him to forgive your mistakes?
2. Why is asking for forgiveness a prayer God loves to hear?

_____

_____

_____

Prayer

LORD, forgive my debts. Amen.

Confessing and Forgiving

If we confess our sins, he is faithful and just and will
forgive us our sins and purify us from all unrighteousness.

– 1 John 1:9

Different Ways to Say "Mistakes"

There are different words for "mistakes" in the Bible. Look at this puzzle.
Find and circle the five words for mistakes.

```
G V D C F A U L T S
T R E S P A S S E S
C V B G V C G I V C
V G T C G V C N G V
M I S T A K E S C G
```

Prayer

Lord, please forgive me when
I make a mistake. Purify my
heart to be more like Your heart.

Amen.

Confessing and Forgiving

If we confess our sins, he is faithful and just and will forgive us our sins and purify us from all unrighteousness.

– 1 John 1:9

A Peek into Your Heart

God looks at your heart all the time. Draw a picture of what He sees there right now.

Prayer

LORD, You see into my heart. Please forgive me for trying to hide my mistakes from You. Help me make right choices. Amen.

Confessing and Forgiving

*If we confess our sins, he is faithful and just and will
forgive us our sins and purify us from all unrighteousness.*

— 1 John 1:9

On Purpose

Sometimes you don't know you are making a mistake. Sometimes you make mistakes on purpose. Do you know the difference? In these five situations, decide if a mistake was an "oops" or if it was done on purpose.

> **1.** Mom tells me it's time for dinner. I don't feel like eating right now so I decide to stay in my room another ten minutes.
>   **This is an "oops"**   **This is on purpose**

> **2.** My brother's lunch bag and my lunch bag look the same. I'm in a hurry leaving for school and accidentally take his lunch bag on the way out the door.
>   **This is an "oops"**   **This is on purpose**

> **3.** I'm tired after my bath. I drop my towel on the floor and leave it there. I don't feel like picking it up.
>   **This is an "oops"**   **This is on purpose**

> **4.** I'm carrying a stack of books for my teacher. I turn the corner in the school hallway and run into Tony and Rick, because I can't see them.
>   **This is an "oops"**   **This is on purpose**

> **5.** I'm mad at Tammi. She waves to me across the cafeteria. I turn away and don't wave back.
>   **This is an "oops"**   **This is on purpose**

Prayer

LORD, sometimes I make a mistake that's an "oops." When that happens, help me see the problem and turn it around. Help me avoid making mistakes on purpose. Amen.

Offering Forgiveness

Forgive as the LORD forgave you.
– Colossians 3:13

Molly's Mess

The kitchen counter was covered with flour. Sugar crunched under Molly's feet. Dirty pans, spoons, and bowls were everywhere. Molly heard her mother's car pull into the driveway. *Uh oh! Mom is not going to like the mess I've made.*

"Molly, what is this?" asked Mom angrily.

"I made brownies," Molly said. "Ben needs to take snacks to preschool tomorrow. You said you didn't have time to make anything." Molly paused. "I'm sorry about the mess."

Mom took a deep breath. "Thank you for helping. I forgive you for making this mess. Now finish the job and clean up, please."

Molly sighed with relief. She washed the dishes, wiped the counters, and swept the floor. She gathered the trash and took it outside. When she came back in, she saw crumbs on the floor.

Ben ran into the kitchen. "I ate a brownie. It was good!"

"I just cleaned up, and you made a mess!" Molly yelled.

Molly's mom forgave Molly's big mess, but Molly didn't want to forgive Ben's little mess. God tells us that He forgives all our sins—our big messes and our little messes.

Your Turn

1. Was Molly fair about giving forgiveness? Why or why not?
2. If it is hard to forgive someone, what can you do?

_____

_____

_____

Prayer

LORD, thank You for forgiving my big messes and little messes. Help me forgive people the way You forgive me. Amen.

359

Offering Forgiveness

Forgive as the LORD forgave you.

– Colossians 3:13

When I Need Help Forgiving

It can be hard to forgive people. In each set of hands, draw a picture or write down a description of a time when it was hard for you to forgive. Tell God about each one. Ask Him to help you forgive.

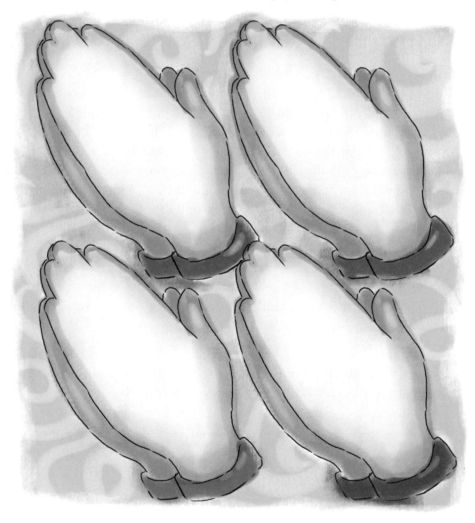

Prayer

Please, God, speak to my heart when I'm mad at someone and don't want to forgive. Help me forgive because I know that's what You desire. Amen.

Offering Forgiveness

Forgive as the LORD forgave you.

– Colossians 3:13

One Reason Why

Sometimes people don't do what we think they should do. We can feel hurt. When we think the person wanted to hurt us on purpose, we are "thinking the worst" about them. "Thinking the best" about someone means you think the person has a good reason for what they did. In each situation, "think the best" about the person. Then write a possible reason they did what they did.

Justin didn't come to church today.
ONE REASON WHY:
_____
_____
_____

My sister has been hogging the bathroom for twenty minutes, and I can't brush my teeth.
ONE REASON WHY:
_____
_____

Dad didn't tuck me into bed tonight.
ONE REASON WHY:
_____
_____
_____
_____

Mrs. Blake, my teacher, didn't smile at all today.
ONE REASON WHY:
_____
_____

Michael usually stands in the lunch line with me. Today he didn't.
ONE REASON WHY:
_____
_____

Prayer

LORD, help me be understanding and think the best about people. Amen.

361

Offering Forgiveness

Forgive as the LORD forgave you.

– Colossians 3:13

Keisha's Grudge

Keisha's family planned to spend Saturday at the lake park. "We'll take a picnic and go swimming," said Dad.

"Would you like to invite Brandy to go with us?" Mama asked Keisha. Brandy was Keisha's best friend. She lived two houses down the street.

Keisha shook her head. She was mad at Brandy. Last Monday, Brandy had ignored her and invited another girl over to her house to play.

"I told Brandy she hurt my feelings last week," said Keisha. "She said she was sorry, but I don't want to forgive her."

Mama nodded. "I see. Do you plan on being mad at Brandy forever?"

Keisha was holding a grudge against Brandy. That grudge was like a wall. It kept Brandy and Keisha having a good time together.

Keisha thought about what Mama said. "I guess forever is a long time to stay mad," she answered. "I'll call Brandy right now."

It's hard to forgive when you are hurt, but when you forgive, you stop feeling angry inside. Don't let a grudge block your way to forgiveness.

Your Turn

1. How do you feel when you hold a grudge?
2. What can you do to let go of a grudge?

_____

_____

_____

_____

Prayer

God, show me how to forgive people and not hold grudges. Amen.

Offering Forgiveness

Forgive as the LORD forgave you.

– Colossians 3:13

Get Rid of Grudges

Keisha learned that a grudge was like a wall that kept her from enjoying her friend. Solve the maze and show Keisha how to get around her grudge and forgive Brandy.

Prayer

LORD, Your Word tells me that if I'm praying and holding a grudge, I need to stop praying, go to the person, work out the problem, and forgive her or him. Help me let go of my hurt and forgive quickly. Amen.

Offering Forgiveness

Forgive as the LORD forgave you.

– Colossians 3:13

Forgiveness Help

When He was on the cross, Jesus said, "Father, forgive them, for they do not know what they are doing" (Luke 23:34). Write down some things people did that Jesus forgave.

_____

_____

_____

Prayer

LORD, help me forgive the people who hurt me. Amen.

Offering Forgiveness

Forgive as the LORD forgave you.

– Colossians 3:13

Who Knows?

Read aloud and write down the rebus clues to find out a great truth. If you need help, read 1 Samuel 16:7.

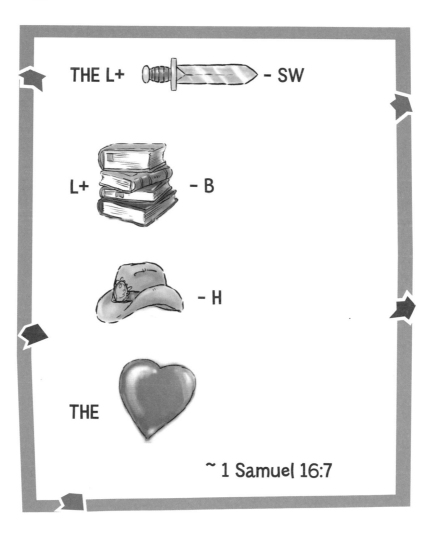

THE L+ [dagger] – SW

L+ [books] – B

[hat] – H

THE [heart]

~ 1 Samuel 16:7

Prayer

LORD, my job isn't to decide if the other person is really sorry or not. My job is to forgive as You have forgiven me. Help me do that. Amen.

God Is Totally Good

Set your heart on the right path.

– Proverbs 23:19

Was It God?

"God tempted me! The chocolate-chip cookies smelled so good, and no one else was around. I ate a whole dozen." *Question:* Does God really want you to get a stomachache?

"God tempted me! I saw my little sister was getting more attention than I was, so I got angry and threw my notebook at her." *Question:* Does God really want you to feel left out?

"God tempted me! I didn't understand three problems on the math test, and I could see Tucker's answers so I copied them." *Question:* Does God really want you to cheat?

God doesn't sit on His throne in heaven all day long thinking up ways to tempt you. He doesn't try to make life hard for you, and He doesn't try to trip you up.

Instead, God wants you to live the right way—His way. It's wrong thinking to believe God tempts you. He wants only the best for you.

Don't blame God when you feel tempted because He never tempts anyone. God is pure good, which makes it impossible for Him to try to trick you or fool you. He loves you and doesn't want you to make mistakes.

Your Turn

1. Why is it easy to think God is tempting you?
2. Why is it wrong thinking to believe God tempts you?

_____

_____

_____

Prayer

God, forgive me for blaming You when I am tempted and when I fail. You are pure goodness and love. Amen.

God Is Totally Good

Set your heart on the right path.

– Proverbs 23:19

God's Thoughts

God wants good for you, not bad. He does not and will not tempt you. Fill in some good thoughts God has for you. If you need ideas, use some of His promises in the Bible. Remember, God can't tempt you to do wrong things because He is only good. He wants to help you do right things.

Prayer

God, when I give in to sin, remind me You are not responsible. I am. Let me turn to You for forgiveness, strength, and guidance. Amen.

God Is Totally Good

Set your heart on the right path.

– Proverbs 23:19

God's Thoughts

To know how to resist temptation, you need to understand when you are being tempted. Do you know when you need to call on God? To test your knowledge, take this mini quiz.

I want to
do something,
even though
I know it's wrong.

☐ **I call on God**
☐ **I do what I want**

I want to do something,
even though it would
mean disobeying my
parents or my teacher.

☐ **I call on God**
☐ **I do what I want**

I want to
do something,
even though I'm
not sure if it's right
or wrong.

☐ **I call on God**
☐ **I do what I want**

Prayer

LORD, remind me to call out to You for help when I'm facing temptation. Give me Your strength to resist. Amen.

God Is Totally Good

Set your heart on the right path.
– Proverbs 23:19

The Pink Sweater

Erin saw the pink sweater in the shop window in the mall. She tugged at her mother's sleeve. "Mom, let's go look in there!" she begged.

The pink sweater was like a magnet. Erin couldn't keep her eyes off it. "This is so tempting," she said as she stood in front of the store staring at the sweater. It didn't matter that she already had eleven sweaters at home in her closet. Erin imagined what she would look like in that sweater. She would be so pretty! And the girls in her class would be jealous. Lexi and Jordan would demand to know where she got the beautiful sweater.

Did God tempt Erin with the sweater? No. God wants Erin to have clothes to wear, but He doesn't want Erin to think only about how she looks or how to make others feel jealous.

Is it wrong to like pretty things? No. But it's important to understand why you want them. You have to be honest with yourself and ask God what He wants for you.

Your Turn

1. Why did Erin want the pink sweater?
2. What are times it's hard to admit that you are wrong?
3. Sometimes we do things for the wrong reason. What helps us know if our reasons are wrong?

_____

_____

_____

Prayer

God, help me be honest and face my temptations with Your eyes and heart. Remind me to call on You for strength, courage, and willingness to follow You. Amen.

God Is Totally Good

Set your heart on the right path.

– Proverbs 23:19

What Pulls You

The pink sweater was like a magnet to Erin—it pulled her in. That's what temptation does. What "pulls you in"? Write down your temptations on the pink sweater. Ask God to help you want the things He wants you to have and to not give in to temptation.

Prayer

LORD, because You are perfect, You never tempt me. Instead, I sometimes get tempted by things I want. Please help me resist in Your name. Thank You. Amen.

God Is Totally Good

Set your heart on the right path.

– Proverbs 23:19

Staying on the Right Path

Solve the rebus to find out how to make good choices and avoid temptation.

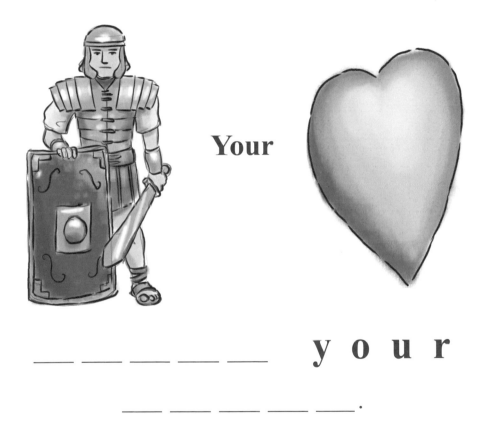

Your

y o u r

___ ___ ___ ___ ___

___ ___ ___ ___ ___ .

~ Proverbs 4:23

Prayer

Lord, help me know what tempts me. Please give me Your strength to avoid it. Amen.

God Is Totally Good

Set your heart on the right path.

– Proverbs 23:19

The Best Way Out

When you face a temptation or a choice, God promises to show you the best way to avoid it. Look at each place. What might tempt Emily in each place? Help Emily avoid deadends and reach the church auditorium.

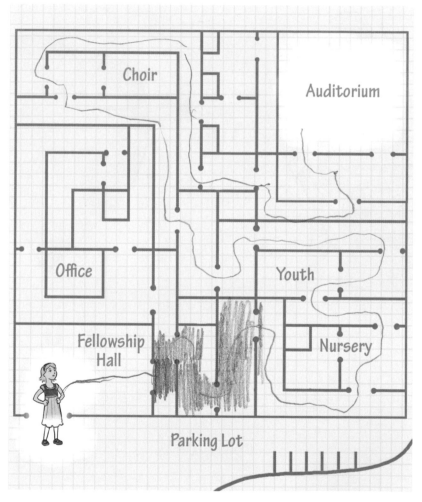

Prayer

LORD, You promised that every time I have a choice and ask You for guidance, You will help me choose the best path. Thank You. Amen.

Answer Key

Page 25

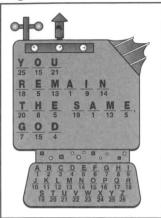

YOU
25 15 21

REMAIN
18 5 13 1 9 14

THE SAME
20 8 5 19 1 13 5

GOD
7 15 4

A B C D E F G H I
1 2 3 4 5 6 7 8 9
J K L M N O P Q R
10 11 12 13 14 15 16 17 18
S T U V W X Y Z
19 20 21 22 23 24 25 26

Page 38

Page 39

911: "Even though I walk through the darkest valley, I will fear no evil, for you are with me; your rod and your staff, they comfort me" (Psalm 23:4).

Page 53
God, My King:
add crowns to (going across) #1, 2, 6

Page 56

Page 57

I will put

God first

Page 70

Page 73

Page 81

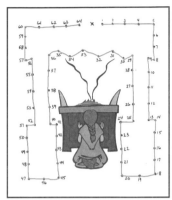

Page 77

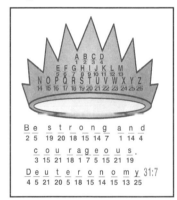

Be strong and
2 5 19 20 18 15 14 7 1 14 4

courageous.
3 15 21 18 1 7 5 15 21 19

Deuteronomy 31:7
4 5 21 20 5 18 15 14 15 13 25

Page 85

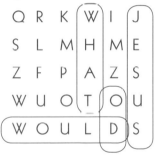

Page 80

Page 104

P R A I S E
1 2 3 4 5 6

THE LORD FOR
7 8 9 10 11 12 13 14 15 16

HE IS GOOD
17 18 19 20 21 22 23 24

Jesus"

Page 140

The Goad Secret: Obey God's goad.

Page 143

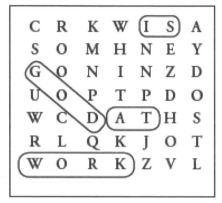

Page 120

Raindrop Scramble: "The LORD is good"

Page 122

Word Puzzle: "Do what is right and good in the LORD's sight."
Deuteronomy 6:18

Page 136

God's Cave Girl: Let us draw near to God with a sincere heart.

Page 139

Heart Puzzle: God loves me!

Page 143

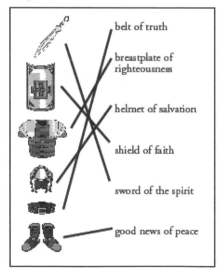

belt of truth

breastplate of righteousness

helmet of salvation

shield of faith

sword of the spirit

good news of peace

Page 139

Buckle Up:
Buckle up with the belt of truth.

Page 181
Knowsy Puzzle:
LORD, You know all things

Page 183
The Fence: mercy

Page 188

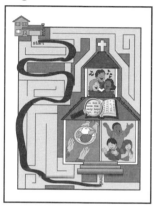

Page 193

Word Keeper: "I am with you always" (Matthew 28:20); "I am the way and the truth and the life" (John 14:6); "I will give you rest" (Matthew 11:28).

Page 206

Page 207

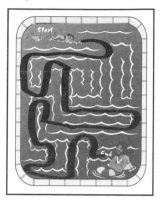

Page 209
My Heart's Eyes: "Love Jesus."

Page 211
Connect the Hearts: "JESUS SAVES"

Page 216

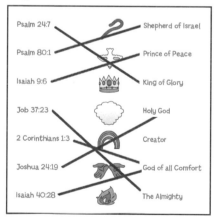

Psalm 24:7		Shepherd of Israel
Psalm 80:1		Prince of Peace
Isaiah 9:6		King of Glory
Job 37:23		Holy God
2 Corinthians 1:3		Creator
Joshua 24:19		God of all Comfort
Isaiah 40:28		The Almighty

Page 224
Forgiveness Steps: God; hurt; Tell; Jesus; go; Jesus; Give.

Page 225

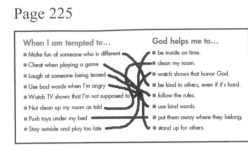

Page 227

Page 244

Page 255

Page 260

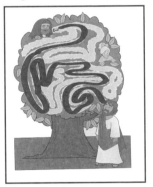

Page 269
My Heart Test:
Pray for the right reasons.

Page 274
One Way to Practice Praying: "Pray continually" (1 Thessalonians 5:17)

Page 283
You Can't Fool God: From the heart

Page 291
The Holy Spirit: Forever!

Page 293

Page 298

Page 300

Page 308
Are You Perfect? Holy One

Page 309

Page 312
Always with Us: Jesus said, "I am always with you."

Page 323
Praising Your King:

Let Israel rejoice in their Maker;

let the people of Zion

be glad in their King.

Let them praise his name with dancing

and make music to him

with timbrel and harp.

Page 325

Page 328
The Right Way:
Teach me to do Your will

Page 329
Plans Puzzle: word search
(purpose, will, ways, plan)

Page 330

Page 340
The Bread of Life: "The one who
comes down from heaven and gives
life to the world" (John 6:33).

Page 342
Types of Rest: drink water, take breaks,
get plenty of sleep

Page 353

Page 354

Page 342
Different Ways to Say "Mistakes":
word search: faults, trespasses,
mistakes, sins, debts

Answer:

G V **D** C **F A U L T S**
T R E S P A S S E S
C V **B** G V **C** G **I** V C
V **G** T C G V C **N** G V
M I S T A K E S C G

Page 363

Page 365
Who Knows? Rebus: "The LORD
looks at the heart" (1 Samuel 16:7).

Page 368
God's Thoughts: I call on God; I call
on God; I call on God

Page 371
Staying on the Right Path: "Guard your
heart" (Proverbs 4:23).

Page 372

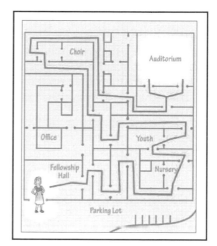

New!

THE GIRL'S GUIDE TO LIFE

Ages 10–12, 192 pages, Paperback, Illustrated.
The Girl's Guide to Life is for girls who want a road map to lead them through life's journey. *The Girl's Guide to Life* points to the Bible, the best map of all, talks about issues girls face like family, friends, boys, school, money, nutrition, fitness, and standing firm when temptations appear. Ages 10–12.

L48220

THE GIRL'S GUIDE FOR PRETEENS

Ages 10–12, 176-208 pages, Paperback, Illustrated.
Encourage girls with these fun and creative books covering issues that matter most to preteens: fashion, being their best, making friends, understanding the Bible, getting along with Mom, dealing with money, and LIFE! Ages 10–12.

L48213

L48211

L48212

L48213

L48214

L48215

L48216

L48217

L48218

L48219

Devotions & Activities for Ages 9-12

L48011

GOD'S GIRLS Fun Crafts Plus Devotions!

Ages 9–12, 184 pages, Paperback, Illustrated. Preteen girls will be captivated by this book, with devotions about Biblical women and crafts created especially for girls. Weaving belts, decorating rooms and party planning activities all teach girls that fun and faith are part of God's plan. Ages 9–12.

THE GOD AND ME!® BIBLE

L48522

Ages 6–9, 192 pages, Paperback, Full Color Illustrations. Designed to capture the vivid imaginations of growing girls, The God and Me! Bible puts God's Word inot the hearts and minds. The bright illustrations, creative activities, puzzles, and games that accompany each Bible story make learning important Bible truths both fun and easy. Ages 6–9.

JUST FOR ME! FOR GIRLS

Ages 6–9, 152 pages, Paperback, Illustrated. Through Stories, crafts, and fun activities, younger girls will discover what they need to grow closer to God! Ages 6–9.

L48413

L48412

L48411

L46911   DB46731

GUIDED JOURNALS FOR GIRLS AND BOYS

Ages 10–12, 136–160 pages, Paperback, Illustrated. Preteen boys and girls will love these daily devotional journals that really encourage them to dig into the Bible.

Ages 6-9 | Ages 10-12

L46971 | L46972

Gotta Have God!
52 Week Devotional for Boys
380–388 pages, Softcover, Full Color Illustrations.

New!

Gotta Have God!

232–248 pages, Softcover, Full Color Illustrations.

Jesus knows all about being a boy because He was one! Jesus knows all about being a boy because He was one! Gotta Have God helps young men learn how much He loves them and wants to be the model for their lives. Each age-based book, for boys ages 2–5, ages 6–9, and ages 10–12, includes devotions and activities designed to help boys understand how they can grow to be strong Christian men. Over 100 devotionals in each book.

L46961 | L46962 | L46963

L46964 | L46965 | L46966

L46967 | L46968 | L46969